Often Christian support for Israe  a theological argument. This bc every generation, brings heart anu personal experience to the issue. If you already love Israel, you'll be encouraged. If you're not sure about God's call for Christians to love Israel and the Jewish people, you'll be moved. Definitely a recommended read.

Rev. Dr. Jim Solberg
USA National Director, BRIDGES FOR PEACE

Every Generation's Story is a must-read for those who want to understand the motives behind the Christian Zionist movement. You will be exposed to firsthand accounts by Christians whose experiences touring Israel transformed them into individuals whose lifework would be to support Israel and the Jewish people. As someone who has worked with the Christian pro-Israel community for over 20 years, I am excited that this book will expose more readers to the genuine and unconditional support for Israel that many Christians share. This will allow for the bond between us to deepen and enable us to work more effectively together to promote our shared Judeo-Christian values and promote Israel through faith-based diplomacy.

Josh Reinstein
President, ISRAEL ALLIES FOUNDATION
Director, KNESSET CHRISTIAN ALLIES CAUCUS

Modern Israel is undeniably a miracle, and one of the often-overlooked aspects of this miracle is the life-changing impact Israel is having on Christians. This book is the testimony of 18 people who will never be the same because of Israel. It is a small sampling of the millions of believers touched by the modern miracle of Israel over the past 75 years. Read it with thankfulness to the Lord for bringing Israel back to life—and be blessed to see how God is working in the lives of others, just as He is doing in your life.

Dr. Jim Showers, DMin, Executive Director/President
THE FRIENDS OF ISRAEL GOSPEL MINISTRY

The big question about our relationship with Israel is whether we are dormant observers or active participants. There is an opportunity here, and the personal anecdotes of the women and men in *Every Generation's Story* tell how they contributed to the narrative of history. In fact, they each authored their own place in the unfolding prophetic message of Israel by showing up and collaborating with my people. I have seen and felt the embrace of our Christian partners in my work at Operation Lifeshield. Our task is to protect lives from enemy rocket attacks by providing secure bomb shelters in vulnerable communities in the Land of Israel. This effort demands help from our closest friends, and their connection to Israel and Israelis is faithful. I loved reading this book because it places a name and face to individuals who answered the call with *hineni*—I am here! And it invites a new generation of Christians to add their story to the telling of Israel's destiny.

Rabbi Shmuel Bowman, Executive Director
OPERATION LIFESHIELD

It is said of King David that he "served the purpose of God in his own generation." That is what this book is all about: powerful testimonies of men and women who understood and served God's eternal purpose with Israel in their own generation. Dr. Susan Michael produced a masterful compilation of testimonies from the Silent Generation to Gen Z. Each story powerfully demonstrates that Israel and the Jewish roots of our faith are relevant in every generation, particularly for the current and future generations. *Every Generation's Story* is a much-needed voice in our time!

Dr. Juergen Buehler, President
INTERNATIONAL CHRISTIAN EMBASSY JERUSALEM

Through her many years of work connecting Christians with Israel, Susan has truly become a pioneer of pioneers, leaving a lasting legacy—an inspiration for us all. Through this book, Susan tells not only her story but the stories of many others who have done the incredible work of ensuring that Christian support for Israel and the Jewish people endures from generation to generation. My prayer is that *Every Generation's Story* serves as a witness of God's amazing faithfulness to His people and encourages a new generation of believers to take up their call to stand with Israel.

Scott Phillips, Chief Executive Officer
PASSAGES

Every Generation's Story: 75 Years of American Christian Engagement with Israel confirms my belief that the Judeo-Christian alliance is the bulwark against the many malign anti-Zionist global forces determined to see Israel destroyed. Beneath this "clash of nations" strategic backdrop is a troubling complex set of antisemitic and anti-Zionist players from the far right to the left, woke, progressive haters. Fortunately, people like Susan Michael and organizations like the International Christian Embassy Jerusalem are front and center in defense of Israel and the Jewish people.

In my novel *Good Heart*, I tell the interwoven story of two families— one Christian, one Jewish, and both supporters of Israel. In her powerful new book, Susan Michael provides 18 *real-life* testimonies that offer fascinating, compelling insights into this righteous pursuit. Read it!

Alan Newman, Author
GOOD HEART

A powerful, wide-ranging collection of stories that shows how Christianity's Hebraic foundations can unify followers of Christ across generations and denominations. An insightful and valuable contribution to the field.

Robert Nicholson, President and Founder
THE PHILOS PROJECT

EVERY GENERATION'S STORY

75 YEARS OF AMERICAN CHRISTIAN ENGAGEMENT WITH ISRAEL

EDITED BY DR. SUSAN MICHAEL

Every Generation's Story: 75 Years of American Christian Engagement with Israel
by Susan M. Michael

Email: embassy.publishers@icejusa.org
Web: www.embassypublishers.org

Embassy Publishers
PO Box 332974
Murfreesboro, TN 37133-2974

Print ISBN 978-0-9839374-8-7
Digital ISBN: 978-0-9839374-7-0

For permissions contact: embassy.publishers@icejusa.org

Editorial: Susan Michael, Tricia Miller; Copyeditor: Karen Engle
Cover design and layout: Peter Ecenroad
Formatting: Nancy Schimp

Printed in the United States of America

—CONTENTS—

—INTRODUCTION—

The US-Israel relationship is not just one of governments but is one found in the hearts of both countries' citizens. American support for Israel at the governmental level largely reflects the millions of Americans who grew up in Sunday School hearing the stories of the heroes of ancient Israel as their own heroes of faith.

Over the last 50 years this relationship has significantly deepened as millions of American Christians have visited Israel. This unique anthology includes testimonies of 18 of them from 5 different generations, all of whom conclude the same thing: Israel changed their lives. Because of their experience in the Holy Land, including getting to know the people of the Land, they returned home with a passion for lifelong engagement.

All Christians who have visited Israel have a story, and most of us have a great one. Therefore, choosing the ones to include in this anthology was not easy. While each story is unique in its own way, these 18 examples truly represent millions of others.

As I began to gather these stories and arrange them in chronological order, two trends became evident. First, Israel's story was surprisingly intertwined with ours. Second, these testimonies did not come from any one organization but represent many of them, thereby demonstrating a national Christian movement in support of Israel.

The representatives of Generation Z do not yet have a life story to tell. Still, they have clearly returned from Israel with the same passion as members of earlier generations who have been involved in long-term work in Jewish-Christian relations, confronting antisemitism, and supporting Israel.

The lesson is clear: we must continue taking Christian young adults to Israel because it will fuel the movement for future generations. It is my prayer that this book will cause every reader—young and old—to want to visit Israel. My second prayer is that it will motivate increased philanthropy to see that happen.

This compilation obviously demands another one be produced to highlight the amazing global story of Christian support for Israel. In the meantime, enjoy reading *Every Generation's Story: 75 Years of American Christian Engagement with Israel.*

Dr. Susan M. Michael
Editor
ICEJ USA Director

THE SILENT GENERATION

Born between 1928–1945

1

A HEART SET ON PILGRIMAGE

JoAnn Magnuson

I am blessed to have spent the first 10 years of my life in my paternal grandmother Ida Emmeline Morgan Gardner's home. Ida, otherwise known as "Gram," was born one year after the end of the American Civil War and died two years after World War II ended. She was a serious student of history and the Bible and a keen observer of the passing scene, my only Christian relative—and my best friend.

My first conscious memory is of the night the Japanese bombed Pearl Harbor on December 7, 1941, declaring war on the United States. I was just four years old, and it was Gram's seventy-fifth birthday. Several relatives had come to the house for dinner and were sitting down to celebrate when a news flash came across the radio. President Roosevelt's familiar voice announced that the Japanese had bombed Pearl Harbor, and we were now at war. My relatives who had sons of draft age began to sob, and the dinner ended quickly. Later that evening as I was helping Gram clean up the kitchen, she put her hand on my shoulder and said, "My dear granddaughter, this will be a terrible war, but Hitler and the Japanese will be defeated, and the Jews will be back in their ancient land. We must pray for that!"

And we did. Gram would often open her Bible and read these verses out loud:

Thus says the LORD, who gives the sun for a light by day, the ordinances of the moon and the stars for a light by night, who disturbs the sea, and its waves roar (the LORD of hosts is His name): "If those ordinances depart from before Me, says the LORD, then the seed of Israel shall also cease from being a nation before Me forever." Thus says the LORD: "If heaven above can be measured, and the foundations of the earth searched out beneath, I will also cast off all the seed of Israel for all that they have done, says the LORD." (Jeremiah 31:35–37)

From December 1941 to the summer of 1945, Gram and I spent most evenings after dinner sitting in front of the big Silvertone radio listening carefully to "war news." Several older cousins were serving in the US military, and we regularly raised prayers on their behalf. Gram faithfully reminded me that "God has a covenant with the Jewish people that will last as long as the sun, the moon, and the stars, and He will bring them back to their ancient land." From her faithful teaching, I gained a sense of personal responsibility for the success of God's restoration project.

When Gram died in May 1947, she left behind her old leather-bound King James Version Bible, in which she had underlined all the promises concerning the restoration of Israel. I poured over that Bible many times the following year, paying particular attention to all the passages Gram had underlined.

Therefore, I was impressed but not too surprised when I came home from school in May 1948 to see the headline of the *Minneapolis Star-Journal* shouting: "State of Israel Declared." I thought, *Wow! Gram knew this would happen because she read the Bible.*

Gram's teaching and this series of events helped form my view of the world and the Bible and set me on a path that led to my lifelong involvement with Israel and the Jewish people.

MY FIRST TRIP TO ISRAEL

In 1977, as my fortieth birthday approached, I prayed about what lessons God might have for me—after all, the number 40 is an important one in the Bible. One morning just before my birthday, the Holy Spirit led me to read Joshua 14:7, a quote from Caleb, Joshua's right-hand man: "I was forty years old when Moses the servant of the Lord sent me ... to spy out the land." I went to Israel for the first time that year, and I have been "spying out the land" ever since by leading 69 tours to Israel.

The group of Lutherans, Catholics, Baptists, and Episcopalians I traveled with in 1977 was a combination of lifelong Bible students and those newly discovering the fun of reading through the sacred text, book by book. The emphasis on the eternal covenant between God and the descendants of Abraham, Isaac, and Jacob took on a clearer sense of importance as we walked the paths and highways of the Land where it all began.

We returned home from that trip with a deeper and more profound understanding of Amos 9:14–15:

"I will bring back the captives of My people Israel; they shall build the waste cities and inhabit them; they shall plant vineyards and drink wine from them; they shall also make gardens and eat fruit from them. I will plant them in their land, and no longer shall they be pulled up from the land I have given them," says the LORD your God.

The continuous relationship of the Jewish people to their ancient homeland is a central theme in Scripture and is often referred to as "Zionism." The movement referred to as "Zionism" represents support of the return of the Jewish people to Zion[1]—the city of Jerusalem and

---

[1] The word "Zion" occurs more than 150 times in the Bible and is synonymous with "city of God," or Jerusalem: "The Lord loves the gates of Zion more than all the dwellings of Jacob. Glorious things are spoken of you, O city of God!" (Psalm 87:2–3). It was initially the ancient Jebusite fortress in Jerusalem, conquered by King David (2 Samuel 5:7), and eventually the seat of power in the kingdom of Israel. Zion also refers to Israel figuratively as the people of God and God's spiritual kingdom.

the Land of Israel—the Land God promised to Abraham and his descendants forever.

The "highway" to God's city—Jerusalem—runs through my heart and the hearts of many Christians. We are not ashamed to be called "Christian Zionists." That term simply means we are Christians who believe that God keeps His promises and that the descendants of Abraham, Isaac, and Jacob are back in their ancient land because God willed it to be so.

Years ago, I stood in front of the Western Wall in Jerusalem with two English friends. I noticed birds nesting in the scrubby vegetation that grows stubbornly from the cracks in those ancient walls. My thoughts turned to the following Psalm:

How lovely is Your tabernacle, O LORD of hosts! My soul longs, yes, even faints for the courts of the LORD; my heart and my flesh cry out for the living God. Even the sparrow has found a home, and the swallow a nest for herself, where she may lay her young— even Your altars, O LORD of hosts, my King and my God. Blessed are those who dwell in Your house; they will still be praising You. Selah Blessed is the man whose strength is in You, *whose heart is set on pilgrimage.* (Psalm 84:1–5, emphasis added)

Indeed, my life has been a pilgrimage as I have set my heart on involvement in the Christian Zionist movement.

One profound experience inspired me to continue my journey on this path. It was in late February 1983, when the spring rainstorms often occur in Jerusalem, and I had just begun to bring American clergy on Familiarization Tours to Israel. Our group had planned to go down to the Dead Sea that day, but on our way, a thunderstorm struck, and we had to turn around and return to our hotel in Jerusalem. Everyone was tired and a bit disappointed over missing a long day at Masada. After assigning everyone to their hotel rooms, I returned to mine and was able to go to sleep.

At about 4:00 a.m., the balcony door in my room started banging— blown open by the wind—and shook me into consciousness. I begrudgingly crawled out of bed and closed the door. What's wrong with this fancy hotel that the outer door won't stay shut?

After it happened three more times, I finally dragged myself out of bed, leaned on the door, and looked out the window heavenward. As I glanced at the sky and the parking lot below me and watched the palm trees blowing over on their sides and the black clouds roiling around in the sky, I said, "Lord, are you trying to tell me something?"

The still, small voice of the Holy Spirit said, "Just wanted you to know what it looks like here, all the time, in the Spirit. There is always a storm raging over Jerusalem. On sunny days you don't notice it. But the enemy of God and man is always at war over Jerusalem. So if you want to teach people to pray and understand Israel, you must know the truth about the battle!"

The longer I've worked in this field, the more grateful I am for that experience.

PIONEERS ON THE ROAD I TRAVELED

My pilgrimage in the field of Christian Zionism brought me into contact with several venerable pioneers in the work. One was G. Douglas Young (1910–1980), who came to Minneapolis in 1953 to teach at Northwestern College. In his studies in the late 1940s and early 1950s, he learned about the horrors of the Holocaust and the disinterest of American churches during and after that atrocity. His scholarly work and life experiences inspired him to become a Christian Zionist.

After becoming dean of the seminary at Northwestern College, he met some Jewish community leaders in Minneapolis. His first trip to Israel in 1956 set him on a course to organize the Institute of Holy Land Studies in Jerusalem, where students from various Christian backgrounds could spend time learning from Jewish and Christian teachers in the land of the Bible. The Institute brought Christian students to the Land to learn Hebrew, study with Israeli archeologists, and go on field trips to map the geography of the Bible. Today this school is known as Jerusalem University College.

Another Christian Zionist pioneer was Rev. Franklin Littell (1917–2009). Rev. Littell visited Germany in 1939, and while there, out of curiosity, attended the Nazi Nuremberg rally. Later in life he recalled being appalled by its open racism and religious glorification of Aryans. When Adolph Hitler made an almost godlike appearance in the stadium, bathed in a halo of lights, Littell was so repelled that he stood up and left the arena.

After the end of World War II, Littell joined the US high commissioner in occupied Germany as the Protestant adviser on de-Nazification. During his subsequent career in education, he started Holocaust studies programs at various colleges and universities, beginning in 1959 at Emory University in Atlanta. At Emory, he set up what may be the first graduate seminar specifically addressing the Holocaust.

I am grateful for Dr. Littell's pioneering work in this field. In the 1950s, when I first began looking for information on the Holocaust, there was little available. Even in the mid-1970s (when I first discovered Littell's *The Crucifixion of the Jews*), a serious student could have read most of the literature available on these topics in a year or so.

As a result of his notable success at starting Holocaust studies programs, Dr. Littell became known as "the father of Holocaust studies." At the same time, he also became an enthusiastic supporter of Israel, partly because he believed Israel's very existence refuted erroneous theologies that foresaw or favored the withering away of the Jewish people. In recent years several of us in the Evangelical world have been invited to participate in Holocaust education seminars at Yad Vashem (the World Holocaust Remembrance Center in Israel). As programs like this continue, our churches and Christian schools will be better equipped to continue the work begun by Rev. Littell and others of that pioneer generation.

In 1978 Rev. Littell, along with Sister Rose Thering and Assembly of God minister Rev. David Allen Lewis, founded the National Christian Leadership Conference for Israel (NCLCI). At its inception, NCLCI lobbied against arms sales to Arab nations that refused to recognize Israel. The organization also actively campaigned against United Nations Resolution 3375, adopted in 1975 and since repealed, that described Zionism as racism.

A third Christian Zionist pioneer I was privileged to know was Rev. David Allen Lewis (1932–2007), chairman of the National Christian

Leadership Conference for Israel. He was an ordained minister in the Assemblies of God and one of the most respected Evangelical voices for Israel. Lewis authored more than 40 books, produced 39 television documentaries on location throughout Israel, and traveled to the Middle East 67 times promoting the welfare of the church, Israel, and the Jewish people.

Rev. Lewis was also a member of the Church Relations Committee of the United States Holocaust Memorial Council. I greatly respect David Lewis as one of the few Evangelicals who was willing to take a chance and work with mainline and Catholic Christians quite early in the development of this movement. It is one thing to show up at an occasional public function and do a "photo op" with people not from your home turf. However, it is quite another to serve on a board for years with church leaders whom many of your church family regard as heretics. Rev. Lewis was a true pioneer in his support for Israel and through his cooperation with a broad swathe of the Christian world.

ORGANIZATIONS I SERVED

In addition to my work with the National Christian Leadership Conference for Israel (NCLCI), which continues to this day, I have worked with the International Christian Embassy Jerusalem (ICEJ), birthed in 1980. My involvement with the ICEJ began when I brought a group of Christians from the United States to the 1981 Feast of Tabernacles. I then volunteered to help open an ICEJ office in the Twin Cities, served as their US prayer ministry director from 1981 to 1985, and worked with them again in 2008–09.

From 1986 to 2007, I served as the US education director for Bridges for Peace (BFP), founded by the abovementioned G. Douglas Young, a Christian Zionist pioneer. I spent over 20 years working for BFP, and these were good years. We had our ups and downs, but I am grateful for the opportunity to have worked with various folks, both Christians and Jews, who saw biblical significance in the rebirth of the State of Israel and were willing to work at supporting it and telling its story.

In addition to my involvement with NCLCI, the ICEJ, and BFP, I have been involved with Christians United for Israel (CUFI) almost since its founding. I continue to serve as CUFI's city director for Minneapolis, Minnesota. I count it a privilege to have been able to donate my personal library of over 2,000 Israel-related books to Maranatha High School, part of Living Word Christian Center in

JoAnn teaching on the Holocaust

suburban Minneapolis, pastored by Mac Hammond, a member of CUFI's executive board.

THE GATHERING OF THE GECKOS

In the Jewish and Christian communities, we activists are always on the lookout for willing volunteers. The need for volunteer laborers reminds me of a Bible teaching I gave some years ago focusing on small creatures and their secrets of success. I had been invited to speak at a Christian women's luncheon and chose this text from the book of Proverbs:

> Four things on earth are small, yet they are extremely wise: *ants* are creatures of little strength, yet they store up their food in the summer; *hyraxes* (or "conies" in the KJV) are creatures of little power, yet they make their home in the crags; *locusts* have no king, yet they advance together in ranks; a *lizard* (or "gecko") can be caught with the hand, yet it is found in kings' palaces. (30:24–28 NIV, emphasis added)

In my talk, I emphasized that God often calls small creatures to do critical work in God's kingdom—and this passage offers hints for success. For example, ants are an example of preparedness and demonstrate why it's crucial to be well prepared in study and supplies to be helpful in the kingdom.

The King James Version describes conies as "feeble folk" who blend into their homes in the rocks and move into strategic positions without being noticed. We, too, can position ourselves strategically by blending in and keeping our eyes, ears, and hearts open.

Locusts advance by sticking together, an example of working collaboratively to advance the kingdom. And finally, *lizards* (or "geckos") are found in kings' palaces. They have feet with suction cup–type features, which make it easy to sneak around in high places without being noticed.

As I lobbied for Israel over the last 40 years in Washington, DC, I have noticed young, seemingly insignificant people serving in the halls of power, many of whom are young Jews and Christians working as interns for congressional officials and government agencies. I think of them as "geckos"—small people in high places. Their names may not appear on the office door, but their work can influence the course of history.

My grandmother used to say, "There is no limit to how much good work you can do, if you don't care who gets the credit."

I suspect that when the tables are laid for the grand banquet on high, there will be a special section for the geckos. And I would be delighted to find my name on that list.

JoAnn Magnuson is an Evangelical Christian who has been involved in a lifetime of support for Israel, teaching on the Holocaust, and building Jewish-Christian relations. She has written various materials on the history of antisemitism and the importance of Holocaust education and, to date, has led 69 study tours to Israel since 1977. JoAnn has served as a consultant and staff member for many pro-Israel Christian organizations, including the International Christian Embassy Jerusalem, Bridges for Peace, Christian Friends of Yad Vashem, Christians United for Israel, and the National Christian Leadership Conference for Israel.

2

THE JOURNEY OF A TRUE FRIEND:
A MAN ON A MISSION

Dr. Marvin Wilson

I was in elementary school during the final years of Adolf Hitler's reign of terror, the last years of the Holocaust and World War II (1939–1945). In those days, there was no television for news reports, and the State of Israel was yet to be born. My first awareness of the Jewish people came from watching short news reels from Europe that played at our local theater on Saturday afternoons. Some reels showed gut-wrenching scenes of Nazis rounding up Jewish people, tormenting them, and destroying their property.

Toward the end of World War II, I was periodically made aware of the suffering of European Jews as my father commented on stories in the *Boston Globe*, delivered daily to our home. However, at this young age, I had no sense of the immensity of the targeting and systematic destruction of the Jewish people. After studying this over my lifetime, I still wonder about the indifference and silence of the church during the Holocaust. Thus, I firmly believe that Christian support of a strong and secure Israel is one important way to right an ugly historical wrong.

My next awareness of the Jewish people came in 1948 after the miraculous birth of the State of Israel. At that time, my pastor, John

Huffman Sr., spent summers in Indiana serving as president of Winona Lake School of Theology. He informed our church that he was about to launch a special summer educational program for seminarians—a "Flying Seminar to Israel"—on the Indiana campus. I remember seeing Rev. Huffman's colorful Israel brochure and watching his slides of the Holy Land as he urged our congregation to pray for this new venture.

In the early 1950s, during my high school years, I went with my parents to several "Israel in Bible Prophecy" conferences held in various New England churches. The speakers affirmed something new and "prophetic" was happening and that it was tied to Israel's return to the Land—the "ingathering" promised in Scripture.

MENTORS IN THE EARLY 1960s

In the winter of 1960, I was in my final semester at Gordon Divinity School and at a crossroads concerning where I should go after graduation. My first inclination was to pursue a degree in New Testament studies because I had been teaching Greek for three years and was assistant to the head of the New Testament department. But I had also taken an intriguing course that piqued my interest in Second Temple Judaism.

The class was an intensive study of the newly discovered Dead Sea Scrolls taught by F. F. Bruce, a world-class New Testament scholar. Simultaneously, my Old Testament professor, Dr. Charles Pfeiffer, encouraged me to pursue graduate studies in Hebrew Bible and Semitic languages. Pfeiffer had studied under Cyrus Gordon, a distinguished Jewish linguist and Hebrew Bible professor. Pfeiffer felt I would thrive under Gordon at Brandeis University, so he drove me there to meet him. Gordon's response to the question about me doing my PhD work under him was, "Yes!"

The following fall, Professor Gordon captured my attention when he started class by saying, "This morning, I would like us to turn to a Torah[2] passage written by my ancestor, Moses." Those words blew me out of the water! No Christian pastor, teacher, or professor I had ever heard spoke

---

[2] *Torah*, a Hebrew word meaning "to teach" or "to instruct," refers to the first five books in the Bible: Genesis, Exodus, Leviticus, Numbers, and Deuteronomy. Both Jews and Christians believe the Torah is the inspired Word of God.

about the Bible in such a personal way. However, as a Jew, Gordon saw himself as part of an interconnected, dynamic family whose teachings and traditions extended back to Sinai.

It was an existential moment that set my life in a new direction. I was studying with one of the "People of the Book," a living scholar linked corporately and spiritually to the greatest Old Testament prophet and teacher—Moses. For the first time in my life, I saw the connection between a historical figure of Israel's past and a living person of Israel's present. Cyrus Gordon's Jewish forebears produced the very book I loved to study and explore. From that day forward, I knew my calling would involve teaching the Hebrew Scriptures and building relations with the People of the Book.

More than 60 years later, I remain puzzled about how Christian scholars, pastors, and teachers can claim to love the Old Testament but have no sense of love, connectedness, indebtedness, or appreciation for the Jewish people—not to mention the Land of Israel. For decades now, I have been a man on a mission to seek and find ways to remedy this disconnect. The Bible is one of the greatest gifts from the Jews, and Christians must find tangible ways to thank the people God chose to impart His revelation to the world. Commitment to involvement in Christian-Jewish relations and support of Israel are meaningful avenues to accomplish this extraordinary task.

DR. G. DOUGLAS YOUNG: EVANGELICAL-JEWISH RELATIONS

After completing my graduate studies at Brandeis in 1963, I started my first full-time teaching position at Barrington College in Rhode Island. During the 1960s, Dr. G. Douglas Young, president of the Institute of Holy Land Studies (now Jerusalem University College), lectured annually at Barrington in my Old Testament classes. While there, Young would recruit students for a summer of study at his Jerusalem campus, established in 1956.

Like Pfeiffer, Young was one of Cyrus Gordon's students. When he spoke, he emphasized why it is important for Christians to visit Israel and why they need to read the Bible through Jewish (non-Western) eyes. As a pioneer in Evangelical-Israeli relations, Young stressed the need for

Christians to return to the source: to study the geographical, archaeological, and physical settings of the Bible in Israel. He also emphasized the need for Christians to learn from and interact with Jewish scholars.

Every time Dr. Young came to Barrington College, he fed a growing hunger within me to visit Israel as soon as possible. I also recognized my need to deepen my understanding of modern Judaism in addition to biblical Judaism. So I began to reach out to rabbis in Providence, Rhode Island, to ask them to lecture in my classes. Many rabbis reciprocated by inviting my Evangelical Christian students and me to their synagogues on *Shabbat*.[3] One rabbi new to the area asked me to read Scripture at his installation service.

For nearly 60 years, my students and I made over 450 field trips into the Jewish community. Each excursion served as a great learning experience and deepened our understanding of Judaism and Jewish communal life. These visitations also provided opportunities to enter respectful, deep conversations with each other. On at least 10 occasions, local synagogues invited my students to present various programs on Shabbat focused on Christian appreciation of Jewish heritage. Likewise, Orthodox, Conservative, Reform, and Hasidic synagogues asked me to be a guest speaker dozens of times.

In June 1967 the Six Day War broke out in Israel. The rabbis of the greater Providence area were greatly concerned about the safety of the Israeli people. One evening, a thousand Jews gathered in the ballroom of a local hotel and pledged over $2.3 million in support of their fellow Jews in Israel. (With inflation, that would be over $10 million today). Dozens of Jewish students in the Brandeis University community also responded to the war in Israel by immediately dropping their studies and catching the next available flight to Israel to help wherever needed so Israelis could join their military units and defend the Land.

These responses to the Six Day War showed me how Jews are an interconnected, international family. They truly care for each other.

---

[3] *Shabbat* is related to the Hebrew verb "cease" or "rest." It is the seventh day of the Jewish week and a day of rest, abstention from work, and celebration that begins on Friday at sunset and ends the following evening after nightfall.

When one Jew suffers pain, all suffer the same pain. Since then I have often wondered if a Christian community 6,000 miles away was in danger and under physical attack, would fellow Christians feel the same urgency and necessity to come alongside and respond as American Jews did for Israel in 1967?

MY FIRST TRIP TO ISRAEL: THE 1972 LOD AIRPORT MASSACRE

In the fall of 1971, I left Barrington College to join the faculty of Gordon College in Wenham, Massachusetts. The following spring, I made my first trip to Israel, where I audited courses and lived in the same building as Dr. G. Douglas Young at the Institute for Holy Land Studies in Jerusalem. He was a helpful mentor as I adjusted to the exciting Jewish culture around me.

However, the day of my arrival in Israel was anything but pleasant. On the contrary, it was shocking, unsettling, and frightening. My flight landed at Lod Airport in Tel Aviv on May 31, hours after a massacre the previous evening in which three terrorists attacked arriving passengers, killing 26 people and wounding 80 others. Israel was still reeling when I arrived, and it was frightening to enter Israel for the first time in this context.

While still in my seat, military and customs officials boarded the plane, frisked me, and inspected each item in my carry-on bags—all while questioning me continuously. Other passengers received similar treatment. When we were finally allowed to enter the terminal, I smelled disinfectant, still pungent after airport workers removed the pools of blood from the terminal floor. I also saw the holes left by the bullets sprayed from the terrorists' assault rifles.

My disconcerting entry into the "Holy Land" remains a powerful reminder of the ubiquitous nature of antisemitism and the fact that Jews are not safe in their own country. The very people who have given so many life-changing blessings and contributions to the world cannot even experience the gift of *shalom* living in their homeland. Little wonder that Israel calls its army the Israel Defense Forces.

What I witnessed in the wake of the massacre at Lod Airport stirred something in my heart. When I started seeing bumper stickers in Massachusetts the following year during the Yom Kippur War (1973) that read, "Burn Jews, Not Oil," I became particularly concerned. I needed to know more about the source of such hatred and violence toward the Jewish people and what Christians could do to help counteract it.

I committed significant time to study antisemitism and the Holocaust and identifying opportunities to educate others. Since the early 1970s, dozens of my students have completed academic internships taught by Holocaust Survivors at the Holocaust Center Boston North. Others have taken leadership roles in speaking out against antisemitism in their communities and through media outlets. A few of my students have held full-time positions with para-synagogue organizations that fight antisemitism. In addition, what I learned from serving on one of the standing committees at the United States Holocaust Memorial Museum in Washington, DC—and from the opportunity to lecture there—was invaluable.

NATIONAL CONFERENCES FOR EVANGELICALS AND JEWS

Several months after I returned from my first trip to Israel, Dr. Young called me from Jerusalem quite unexpectedly. He had recently visited New York and had a lengthy conversation with one of the most influential rabbis in America, Rabbi Marc Tanenbaum, director of interreligious affairs at the American Jewish Committee. Tanenbaum emphasized to Young that in the States, Jews and Evangelical Christians do not know or understand each other well and that he would like to see that situation change. Tanenbaum asked Young about developing a three-day conference that would feature a dialogue between Evangelical and Jewish scholars and leaders. Young's Institute for Holy Land Studies and the American Jewish Committee (AJC) would cosponsor the conference. Young needed to remain in Israel, so he asked if I would be willing to serve as the Evangelical coordinator of the conference. I would be working with Tanenbaum and his staff to develop the program and secure the most knowledgeable Evangelical scholars to speak on the topics agreed upon for the conference. With some trepidation, I accepted the assignment, which involved three years of planning in cooperation with AJC staff.

The first conference ensued in New York City from December 8 to 10, 1975. In 1980, 1984, and 1995, I was invited to lead three more conferences for Evangelicals and Jews. In addition, I was privileged to coedit with Rabbi James Rudin four published volumes containing the addresses presented at those conferences. These national meetings proved that Evangelicals and Jews could successfully conduct constructive conversations on Scripture, theology, history, Israel, the Holocaust, atonement, redemption, Messiah, and more.

In 1989 I published *Our Father Abraham: Jewish Roots of the Christian Faith* (William B. Eerdmans), a textbook on the relationship of Judaism to Christianity and the history of Christian-Jewish relations. After more than 30 printings and translations into six foreign languages, a second (expanded) edition of the book was released in 2021. Connecticut Public Television coproduced an award-winning two-hour national television documentary, *Jews & Christians: A Journey of Faith* based on *Our Father Abraham,* now available on DVD, for which I was privileged to serve as the primary scholar.

I am indebted to Dr. G. Douglas Young for how in my formative years as a scholar, he instilled confidence in me that Evangelical-Jewish relations were possible. He emphasized the importance of including Evangelical and Jewish perspectives on Israel in conference agendas and insisted that sensitive and patient dialogue could be productive and exceedingly valuable. He was right! My decades of experience focused on Evangelical-Jewish relations testify to Dr. Young's vision and wisdom. When this distinguished leader passed away in 1980, he left a great legacy. May his memory always be a blessing.

RETURN VISITS TO ISRAEL HAVE CHANGED MY LIFE

When my first visit to Israel ended and it was time to return home, I was overwhelmed with sadness. As I boarded my flight back to the States, one question consumed me: How soon could I return? The Land has such a powerful attraction. There is so much to learn and explore. The educational, historical, and spiritual riches available in Israel are inexhaustible. After nearly 30 return trips, my fondness for and friendship with Israel and its people has continued to grow. What follows are a few (of many) ways Israel has changed my life.

First, I read the Bible differently. As a Western Bible teacher, I recognize the Bible as an Eastern book that must be understood through Eastern, Semitic eyes. Being in Israel allowed me to see the difference. The Land offers rich commentary on Scripture through its geographical, topological, and archaeological setting. While exploring the biblical sites, I quickly became aware of how the location of roads, hills, valleys, and water within modern Israel parallels the ancient. Being in the Land also greatly enlarged my understanding of the life and humanity of Jesus.

Second, my life has been changed through the joy of encouraging others to experience Israel. Over the years, dozens of my students studied at Jerusalem University College. Others became fluent in Hebrew while earning graduate degrees in Second Temple Judaism at Hebrew University in Jerusalem. A few students have volunteered on *kibbutzim*,[4] and some have pastored congregations in Israel. I have led over a thousand American Christians from various denominations on tours to Israel after teaching seminars to prepare them for the experience of a lifetime.

Third, Israel provided the opportunity to expand my work in Evangelical-Jewish relations. I have spoken at synagogues and churches in Jerusalem and conferences sponsored by the International Christian Embassy Jerusalem (ICEJ). I co-led an interfaith trip with a Conservative rabbi friend, and upon returning home, this same interfaith group celebrated *Shavuot*[5] (Pentecost) together. I have also served on the Advisory Boards of the Institute of Holy Land Studies (IHLS), Jerusalem University College (the former IHLS), Bridges for Peace, and the ICEJ.

The largest and most challenging audience in Israel I was invited to address was an international interfaith conference at the Jerusalem Convention Center. Several thousand Jewish and Christian leaders from

---

[4] *Kibbutzim* (plural) are collective Israeli settlements. In a *kibbutz* (singular), all income generated by its members goes into a common pool. Kibbutzim have historically been involved with Aliyah and building the country.

[5] *Shavuot*, or the "Feast of Weeks," is one of the three biblically ordained pilgrimage festivals in the Bible (see Leviticus 23). This Jewish holiday occurs today between May 15 and June 15 on Gregorian calendars; in biblical times, it marked the wheat harvest in Israel (Exodus 34:22).

97 nations attended. I was surprised when a group of Orthodox Jews blocked the auditorium entrance in a "sit-down" protest, angered that Jews would dialogue with Christians. Police carried the protesters out before I was allowed to speak on Evangelical-Jewish relations. Sharing the platform with me that afternoon were Archbishop of Canterbury George Carey and Joseph Ratzinger, a Catholic cardinal who a decade later was elected Pope Benedict XVI. My address was carried around the world on BBC radio.

As I stood before this incredible audience, I silently thanked God that my first awareness of the new State of Israel in Pastor Huffman's church in 1948 had come full circle. Yes, the protestors' distracting presence reminded me of the fragility of interfaith dialogue. But despite the obstacles, I knew in my heart it was the road for me to travel. I also realized God allowed me the privilege of being in that Jerusalem venue so I could present the critical necessity of Evangelical-Jewish relations. Indeed, it was—and is—a challenge heard by religious leaders worldwide. To God be the glory for the work He has done and continues to do!

Marvin R. Wilson, PhD, is a leading scholar on Christian-Jewish relations. He is the Harold J. Ockenga Professor Emeritus of Biblical Studies at Gordon College, Wenham, Massachusetts, where he taught for more than 50 years. He is the author of the widely used text Our Father Abraham: Jewish Roots of the Christian Faith. *Wilson served as the primary scholar for the award-winning national television documentary* Jews & Christians: A Journey of Faith, *based on* Our Father Abraham.

BABY BOOMERS

Born between 1946–1964

3

A MAN ALWAYS RETURNING

Dr. John Swails

The first time I remember thinking about the modern State of Israel was when I was about 10 years old. I remember flipping through a new encyclopedia set my parents had purchased and seeing the entry for Israel with a picture of an Israeli army jeep. I asked my folks about it, and they reminded me that they had told me about the recent establishment of the Jewish State. Clearly, it took some time for that reality to register in my mind.

For some time, my interest did not extend beyond a passing curiosity, despite news items and current events concerning Israel. The next step in the development of my engagement with Israel came when I was 13. In February 1962 Oral Roberts came to our home in Franklin Springs, Georgia, to recruit my father as one of the founding faculty members of a new university he was establishing in Tulsa, Oklahoma. At one point, he gathered my parents, my two brothers, and me in our living room to present what he envisioned for the university now known as Oral Roberts University (ORU). I remember two points he made that day: First, that ORU would have a national championship basketball team, and second, a branch of the university would be established one day in Israel. After his visit, my dad told me about several other times Oral had spoken about his desire to do something in and for Israel. In retrospect, considering these experiences, it seems odd that I continued to be unconcerned about Israel and its people—and the plans of the Almighty for the same. But at that point in my life, I was building (or attempting to build) my own kingdom, and the Lord was not part of those efforts.

In 1964 my father made his first trip to Israel. He returned with impressions that solidified into a firm conviction: he would not rest until he had taken his whole family to Israel. In short, he accomplished this— and so much more.

My father's commitment to bringing his family to Israel led to plans for a tour that would include my mother and me. Our departure date was to be June 5, 1967. That became a historic day for the State of Israel as it was the start of the Six Day War. My mom woke me up that morning with the news that war had broken out in the Holy Land, so our trip was canceled. Since it was uncertain whether the tour could be rescheduled that year, I enrolled in summer school at the University of Georgia. Subsequently, when it did become possible for the group to go in July, I was in class and could not join them.

Dad had persuaded our next-door neighbor, John Noseworthy, to lead that first tour. It was so successful—despite the circumstances—that John and my dad planned another trip for the summer of 1968. John was a gifted man who worked at an advertising job that paid poorly and did not challenge him. I remember my dad telling John that he was a natural for the travel business. He frequently exclaimed, "John, you can do this!"

John ended up leading two tours to Israel in the summer of 1968. He eventually left his job to go into the travel business and started his own company, Noseworthy Travel, which is still in business. Before his death, John took almost 70,000 people to Israel, earned two gold medals from the Israel Ministry of Tourism, and traveled there about 250 times.

My first trip to Israel was an expedition that took three weeks, covered fourteen different countries, and included eight days in Israel—a tour led by my father and John Noseworthy. My roommate was my good friend from Franklin Springs, A. D. (Doug) Beacham, Jr. Doug and I set off with great excitement in anticipation of an epic tour. Our group went through Europe to Moscow and then to Cairo, Egypt. But when attempting to depart Egypt from the old Cairo West Airport, we learned that our flight to Beirut, Lebanon, had been canceled because the "omens were wrong." While waiting in the desert airport for several hours in the heat without bottled water, we became desperate for some form of hydration.

Fortunately, a vendor passed by with a cart full of ice and oranges; we all bought fresh orange juice, which was incredibly sweet and refreshing. However, we soon began to pay the price for that refreshment as gastrointestinal distress afflicted members of our group in quick succession. My symptoms started during the flight from Beirut to Cyprus, and by the time we flew from Cyprus to Israel, I was suffering and feeling quite sorry for myself. As we approached Israel, I was dozing while still aware of my pain and abdominal distress.

However, as soon as the plane touched down at Lod Airport, it was as if a mild electrical charge zapped me; I still recall the intense sensation vividly, even today. I sat up and looked around, my symptoms began to recede, and a sense of excitement and enthusiasm replaced my focus on my physical issue. *I am in Israel. I've come home!* I thought. I continued to marvel at that fact for the rest of that trip—and every time I have spent time in the Land since.

A STILL SMALL VOICE

At one point during that first trip to Israel, we had a free day in Jerusalem. My dad asked what I wanted to do with the time. I had been impressed by the Hebrew University campus during our brief visit during the tour, so I told my dad I wanted to revisit it.

As we walked from the bus stop onto the campus, the words came into my mind: "Why don't you come back here next year as a student?" I repeated those words to my dad, who responded positively, and the next thing I knew, we had detoured to the office for overseas students and started the process that would bring me back to the Land in 1969. It was a complex process in those days, especially compared to the relatively easy process students go through today to study in Israel.

Back home, I applied to several graduate schools where I could study the Ancient Near East—the context in which the Bible was written. I was accepted and received offers of fellowship money from more than one. However, when I visited the school making me the best offer, I realized it was not the right school for me. I then met with my dad at a camp meeting where he was speaking, and as we walked and talked, he turned to me and said, "It looks like you should go to Hebrew University." I nodded, and it was settled. They had offered generous funding for the Summer Ulpan, where I would learn modern Hebrew, so it was now just a matter of preparing for the trip.

However, before preparing for the trip, I had to deal with what could have been a significant complication. I was engaged to be married to Joy Williams from North Carolina, and I now had to explain this decision to her. To her lasting credit, she received the news well and encouraged me in my course. The same Spirit was leading her as me, and this mutual leading has continued to mark our relationship as we have been married for over 50 years. Joy's commitment to the leading of the Spirit and Israel would be a vital part of our lives and would even include giving birth to one of our children in Jerusalem.

John at the port of Tel Aviv, 2011

THE HOMELAND OF MY HEART

Off I went to Hebrew University with a group sponsored by the American Friends of Hebrew University. When I met the other 400 students at an orientation in New York City, I realized they were all Jewish. It would be several weeks into our stay in Israel before I discovered three other Christians in the group. Finally, after two days of meetings in New York City, we boarded the plane for Israel, arriving late in the afternoon. We descended onto the tarmac at Lod Airport to retrieve our luggage, and after locating my suitcase, I sat down on the concrete to wait.

Soon students started protesting that busses were not waiting for us upon our arrival. Amid the turmoil, an Israeli *madrich* (counselor) walked up and spoke in Hebrew. I looked at him for explanation, and he said: "Don't worry–you are home." I can't describe the effect those words had on me—I can still feel it. All the noise and confusion receded into the background, and a sense of peace and belonging settled in—a sense quite real even today. People said the madrich must have thought I was Jewish when he said I was home, but that doesn't matter to me. His words dug into my heart and have remained lodged there ever since. They are the reason I teach students to learn about and travel to Israel. I tell my students: "Israel is the homeland of your heart, and it is also the frontline of history."

We eventually boarded buses and headed off into the desert. Our dormitories in Jerusalem were incomplete, so we began our language studies at a *midrasha* (institute for Torah studies), which was located next to Kibbutz Sde Boker where David Ben-Gurion, the first prime minister of Israel and an important world figure in the twentieth century, lived in retirement. We often saw him on his morning and evening walks around the kibbutz and midrasha grounds, always accompanied by his four-man security detail.

We arrived at the midrasha for the first time at 10:30 p.m. and were shown to our rooms, located around a plaza within a compound. I found myself in a room with four young Jewish men from large cities in the northern United States, while I was from a small southern town of fewer than 500 people—and obviously not Jewish. Nonetheless, that night began an exciting and enjoyable time of cultural exchange and the formation of friendships that exist to this day.

LEARNING FROM BEN-GURION

I had the opportunity to hear Ben-Gurion speak on more than one occasion. He was 83 at the time and still walking vigorously every morning and evening for considerable distances. His mind was exceptionally sharp, and his remarks and interactions with people and their questions impressive. When students with different views asked him about historical events, he answered while motioning with his characteristic chopping-hand movement you can still see in videos from throughout his life.

What impressed me most was the fire that still burned inside him. That "fire" propelled him through difficult and dire situations, fueled his immense energy and courage, and undergirded his vision for Israel. Undoubtedly, meeting and hearing from David Ben-Gurion was transformative in my life.

Ben-Gurion's vision for Israel was biblically based. He believed the prophet Isaiah's words that Israel was to be "a light for the nations" (Isaiah 49:6 ESV). I heard him say this several times and always with the same conviction and confidence. He had an appreciation and respect for Scripture that went beyond his contemporaries and guided his thinking and life. I believe he would be pleased to see how Israeli innovations in science, medicine, and technology benefit the world today.

Ben-Gurion was also committed to settling the desert, and he emphasized that commitment every time I heard him speak—and it's also why he retired and chose to be buried there. He would have been overjoyed to witness the signing of the Abraham Accords II at Sde Boker Kibbutz in the spring of 2020. So as often as I can while in Israel, I visit his grave at Sde Boker and put a stone of remembrance on his cover stone to pay respects to a great human being whose impact on my young life has only increased with time.

A LIFELONG PASSION

Ever since my first trip to Israel as a teen, my life has been focused on Israel, the Jewish people, and the Almighty's love for His people. My 40 trips to the Land—twice for extended periods (one of which included the birth of our youngest son, Joel, in Jerusalem)—have only intensified that focus.

Yet through the years, I've wondered about the strangeness of it all. Though I periodically questioned whether I should alter the direction of my life, I relate to the apostle Paul's words: "I was not disobedient to the heavenly vision" (Acts 26:19). My work has always been motivated by an irresistible call and vision from God—and because of this, it will always focus on Israel.

As a professor of history and government and the director of the Center for Israel and Middle East Studies at ORU, I have taught well over a thousand students about the history and significance of Israel. I have traveled to Israel 40 times, 17 of which were study trips. I have also served several pro-Israel organizations in an advisory capacity, such as the International Christian Embassy Jerusalem (ICEJ), Christians United for Israel (CUFI), and the American Israel Public Affairs Committee (AIPAC).

And although I love teaching, I am always ready to return to Israel. The refrain of an Israeli song by Yehoram Gaon says, "I am the man who is always returning." Those words have become my life motto.

John W. Swails III, PhD, is the director of the Center for Israel and Middle East Studies at Oral Roberts University in Tulsa, Oklahoma. He has degrees from the University of Georgia in Modern Jewish History and the Modern Middle East and from Brandeis University in Ancient Near East Studies. He teaches courses on modern Israel, World War II and the Holocaust, the Ancient Near East, radical Islam, and the Islamic Middle East.

4

STEPPING INTO HISTORY

Susan Michael

When I was a teenager, I hated history and, as a result, knew little of it. I also avoided studying languages and justified it by thinking I would never leave the United States. But God had His plans, and by the time I was 19, I was already on my way overseas to Israel, where I would study Hebrew and become fascinated with history. Little had I known what was ahead for me.

I was a biblical studies major at Oral Roberts University (ORU) when I met others on campus who had studied abroad the previous summer. I thought that sounded like fun, so I asked one of my professors, Dr. Roy Hayden, if he knew of any study programs in Israel. He enthusiastically responded, "Absolutely! And go, if possible, because it will change your life."

Unbeknownst to me, I had picked the one professor in the entire university who had a relationship with a small Christian school in Jerusalem called the Institute of Holy Land Studies (now called Jerusalem University College). Dr. Hayden knew what he was talking about. My time studying in Israel made the Bible come alive—it went from being two-dimensional to three-dimensional—and was a life-changing experience that ignited my faith and brought greater passion and purpose to my life.

But that was only the beginning. I was about to step into two moments in history that would become intricately woven into the tapestry of my own life and story.

I landed at Ben Gurion Airport for that summer study program in 1978 knowing nothing about Israel or the Middle East. All I knew was that Israel was the land of the Bible. I did not know the Jewish State had not existed for close to 2,000 years or about the defensive wars the reestablished State had to fight with their Arab neighbors in 1948, 1967, and 1973 or that historic peace talks were taking place that summer between Israel and Egypt.

I certainly had no idea my life would soon become intertwined with both Israel and Egypt. Looking back, God indeed had a sense of humor to have taken this young girl from a rural community in Kentucky and set her down in the middle of the Arab Israeli conflict and Jewish-Christian relations. But that is precisely what He was doing.

During my five-week study program, I took one course called "Historical Geography of the Bible Lands," where I studied with the Bible in one hand and a map in the other. After studying about a particular region in class, we would board a bus and go to the actual site. This experience transformed how I read the Bible and developed my love for maps! The second course was "Modern Israeli Society," which I found fascinating. It introduced me to the Jewish faith and the diverse mosaic of Israeli society.

Susan on Mount Zion in 1978

I loved these courses and wanted more! So after I finished my bachelor's degree at ORU, I returned to the Institute in 1980 to pursue a master's degree. The small school only had three degree programs, and I was not interested in Hebrew language or archaeology. So that left the degree called Judeo-Christian Studies. Choosing that course of study was proof that I had no career plans! But it was undoubtedly God's choice for my life. It was an excellent introduction to the history of Judaism, Christianity, and Islam—as well as the modern history of the Middle East.

GOD'S PERFECT TIMING

The timing of my studies in Israel placed me in the center of a historic moment that was far more significant than the courses themselves. In the summer of 1980, the Israeli Knesset passed the Jerusalem bill, establishing all of Jerusalem as the eternal, undivided capital of the State of Israel. There was a considerable uproar about this in the Arab world, which responded by threatening oil embargos on any country that recognized Jerusalem as the capital of Israel. It was a traumatic moment for Israel when all foreign embassies in Jerusalem moved out to avoid recognizing the city as the capital.

At the same time, there was a prayer group of Christian leaders from several different countries who were living in Jerusalem at the time. They had been praying about two things—one of which was to begin celebrating the biblical Feast of Tabernacles.

Few Christians in the 1970s were aware of the meaning of this biblical Feast or that the prophet Zechariah foretold that all nations would one day celebrate it. These visionaries in Jerusalem felt they needed to bring an understanding of the holiday to churches around the world. So they organized the first international Christian celebration of the Feast of Tabernacles in Jerusalem, held one month after I arrived.

The second idea this group of leaders had was to create a Christian organization in support of Israel. The director of the Institute at that time, Dr. George Giacumakis, was one of those leaders, and it is thanks to him I knew about these developments and was privileged to be involved.

I also have Professor Ray Pritz of the Institute to thank for his role. During my first week of classes, he called three of us aside and asked if we wanted to start an Intercessors for Israel prayer group. We said yes and invited another student, Timothy (Tim) King, to join us. During our first prayer meeting, Dr. Pritz met with us to teach us about prayer. Before our prayer group met on its own the following week, Dr. Giacumakis had asked Tim to be the financial director of the new organization they were starting— the establishment of which would be announced at the Feast of Tabernacles event. His decision became our first prayer request.

The Feast celebration took place at the Anglican School, and some 1,500 Christians from over 15 countries attended. During the event, the organizers announced they did not support the evacuation of embassies from Jerusalem and were opening an international Christian embassy in Jerusalem. This Christian embassy would represent the millions of Bible-based Christians around the world who understood the significance of Jerusalem to the Jewish people and stood with Israel in making it their capital city.

These bold leaders launched the International Christian Embassy Jerusalem (ICEJ) from an empty three-bedroom apartment for an office and without a penny in the bank. The receptionist sat on a suitcase with an old black rotary dial phone in her lap! And I stood in the front yard with a backpack on my back, witnessing history in the making.

Little did I know God was also launching my personal destiny that day.

Dr. Giacumakis became the founding chairman of the board, Tim the financial director, and our little prayer group focused on the birth pangs of the ICEJ. During one of our meetings, we were praying about opening a branch in the United States, and Tim mentioned they wanted the head office to be in Washington, DC. During that time of prayer, I knew God was calling me to Washington, DC—a city I had never been to and one in which I knew no one.

A few weeks later, one of the founders of the ICEJ, Jan Willem van der Hoeven, asked me what I was planning to do once I finished my degree. I said, "I don't know, but I think I am supposed to go to Washington, DC." He excitedly threw his arms in the air and said, "We just returned from DC, where we met with the head of the American Israel Public Affairs Committee—AIPAC. You must go and work with AIPAC on our behalf!" A proposal was sent to Tom Dine, AIPAC's executive director, who agreed to take me on for six months as an intern. I moved to DC in 1983 and remained there for 29 years, where I helped establish the USA Branch of the ICEJ. This is also where I met my husband.

THE EGYPTIAN CONNECTION

This brings me to the second historic moment I had stepped into when I first went to Israel. As soon as Israel and Egypt signed a peace treaty in 1979, tourism opened between the two countries, and a steady flow of Israeli tourists began visiting Egypt. A fellow student, Marta Rios [Escarcega] from California, and I went to Egypt with one of those groups. We traveled by bus from Jerusalem through the hot, dusty Sinai to Cairo—a 10-hour ride!

My sinuses are sensitive to dust, so by the time we arrived in Cairo, my head felt several times bigger than it should have. After we checked in at the St. George Hotel across from the Cairo Zoo, I asked at the front desk where I could find a pharmacy and was given easy directions to one nearby. It was dusk as I made my way across a huge highway full of cars to enter that pharmacy.

At the time, I didn't know that the man God had destined me to marry was an Egyptian pharmacist named George Michael (*Mikhaeel* in Arabic), and most late afternoons, he was in that pharmacy. In a city of 18 million people and thousands of small pharmacies, that front desk agent had sent me to the one owned by the father of George's good friend from pharmacy school. It was in a medical building that George frequented as a pharmaceutical sales rep, so he would often visit his friend in the late afternoon. While there he would help wait on customers, many of whom were tourists.

I remember a kind, handsome young man waited on me, but for years was not sure if it had been George or his friend. Then one day, after we had been married for 34 years, George asked me if the young pharmacist had been thin or heavy. When I said he was thin, he said, "That was me. I was pencil-thin back then, and my friend was very heavy." This chance encounter had not been chance at all! A mighty God had orchestrated the whole sequence of events!

Interestingly, George also met some of the many Israeli tourists visiting Egypt at that time. He had grown up during the antisemitic government of Gamal Abdel Nasser, but his mother had told him not to believe what he heard about Jews because they were nice people. He now experienced that for himself. His new Israeli friends even invited him to their home, and he was one of the few Egyptians who visited Israel as a tourist then.

A few years later, George and I met for the second time—this time on the other side of the world at a church in Washington, DC. When he heard of my interest in the Middle East, he wanted to know why, and his first question was what I thought about Israel. I said, "I love Israel. I lived there for two years." He said, "Good. Me too." I passed the test, and we were married in 1988.

I could never have done what I have for Israel had it not been for George's continuous support. The Middle East is a complex arena made up of issues that are a mix of historical, cultural, and religious elements. George's knowledge, biblical worldview, and insight into current events informed me—and gave me great confidence in my calling.

George and I share a love for the Jewish people and a love for the Arabs, and we have continuously endeavored to bring this into the teaching and message of the ICEJ. We appreciate the special, biblical calling on the Jewish people to bless the world with God's redemptive plan and know that He chose them and initiated His plan because of His love for *all* people. God's choice of the Jewish people was for the sake of a world He loves.

CONNECTING AMERICAN CHRISTIANS TO ISRAEL

I am so grateful for the role Israel has played in my life—it literally opened the world to me and was a stepping stone into an appreciation of history, cultures, and world affairs. My Bible became what I call "the most exciting book on the planet." In return, I have done—and continue to do—everything I can to connect Christians with Israel so they can have this same experience.

In the early years of building the USA Branch of the ICEJ, we organized large Feast-type events and conferences across the United States attended by some 20,000 people each summer. We hosted the Washington for Israel Summit in DC in 1992, the first major pro-Israel Christian conference of its kind in the United States. In the early 2000s we began focusing more on educating churches and developed several half-day seminars and small group study series for them. The feedback we received confirmed the need to put even more effort into building educational resources.

In response to this need, we built the Israel Answers website to present the facts about Israel, Christian Zionism, and antisemitism. We now offer online courses under the banner of ICEJ U and are developing course curricula that can be taught for credit in Christian colleges. In addition, we lead an array of study tours to Israel for pastors, young adults, and churches and are publishing books like this one under the imprint Embassy Publishers.

After years of collaboration with other leaders in Washington, DC, we formed a powerful network of Christian leaders who not only speak *for* but *to* tens of millions of Americans. The American Christian Leaders for Israel (ACLI) network has carried out a number of joint initiatives and events. Another facet of my work in DC was that I had the joy of pioneering Evangelical-Jewish relations. I spoke in synagogues and to many Jewish audiences and assisted Jewish organizations—including the Embassy of Israel—as they sought to build relations with Christians.

We did all of this while raising funds for our ICEJ headquarters' projects in Israel—including assisting over 170,000 Jews in making Aliyah[6] to Israel, sponsoring the largest home for Holocaust Survivors in Israel, and placing more than 180 bomb shelters that bring security and peace of mind to many Israeli communities. Over the years, the ICEJ has blessed every village and sector of Israeli society.

---

[6] *Aliyah* is derived from a root Hebrew word that means "going up," "to ascend," or "elevation." In the Jewish community, Aliyah can mean the act of being called forward to read the Torah in the synagogue. However, it has also come to refer to when a Jewish person immigrates to the Land of Israel.

THE PRIVILEGE OF A FRONT ROW SEAT

I am so thankful for that prayer group of visionaries in Jerusalem who, in 1980, birthed a unique, global organization that currently has a presence in over 90 countries of the world. At the same time, they birthed an awareness of the biblical Feast of Tabernacles, which is now celebrated annually by thousands of Christians in Jerusalem and in many churches worldwide. Though the fulfillment of Zechariah's prophecy is for a future era, we are practicing for it now and preparing the way for amazing days to come.

I am equally thankful to have been born in this generation and to witness the miraculous return of the Jewish people to their ancient homeland. We are watching prophecy be fulfilled and rejoice in the faithfulness of God to His Word. To be on the front lines of what God is doing in Israel and around the world is a privilege and a blessing.

When I was a student in Jerusalem, my address was PO Box 1276, Mount Zion. That is where God changed my life and where my heart remains—in Zion!

Dr. Susan Michael is the ICEJ USA Director of the International Christian Embassy Jerusalem and has been a pioneer in furthering Christian engagement with Israel and the Jewish people for more than four decades. She is an author, gifted teacher, and international speaker. Her experience, studies, and travel to Israel over the past 45 years have equipped her to handle complex issues surrounding biblical and modern Israel with extraordinary clarity and grace. She is the author of Encounter the 3D Bible: How to Read the Bible So It Comes to Life.

5

TRUST AND OBEY

Timothy King

The Vietnam war was raging. I was an American living in Toronto, Canada, and everyone thought I was a "draft dodger!" Though not the case, I could hardly convince anyone differently. The reality was that I moved to Canada because of my position as merchandise manager of the Canadian Retail Division of Goodyear Tire and Rubber Company. Such was one of the challenges the American "boomer generation" faced in the 1970s.

At that time, I had never met a Jew, never thought about Israel, and had no idea how insidious antisemitism was.

But that all changed in 1978. I was preparing to be a volunteer for a Billy Graham event in Toronto when a preacher asked, "Have you ever considered going back to school?" I was shocked! He had no way of knowing that I had a marketing degree from Kent State University in Ohio, as he had never met me before asking this question. I looked him in the eye and answered no—I had never considered returning to school. "That is," I said, "until a few moments ago during your sermon when God 'spoke' to me."

This preacher had no idea I was utterly ignorant concerning Israel and the Jewish people, of God's eternal purposes for Israel, and of my Christian responsibility to stand with this ancient people. But God had a plan, and I was to be part of it.

"I have just the school for you," he said. He proceeded to write a letter of introduction to the Institute of Holy Land Studies on Mount Zion, Jerusalem. And in 1979 I went there to pursue a master's degree in Judeo-Christian Studies.

Being born into the "boomer" generation meant I grew up in the most exciting, freeing, and challenging time possible. World War II was over, and we "boomers" were the product of that freedom. However, amid all the freedom, we also had the materialism of that generation and the Vietnam war to contend with, each in our own way.

HOW THIS BOOMER GOT TO ISRAEL

I was born October 2, 1946, as the second son of three to the late Reuben and Mary Jane King. I was the 55th of 59 grandchildren on my father's side, whose family immigrated to Philadelphia, Pennsylvania, from the Alsace German Swiss part of Europe in 1740 in search of religious freedom. They were Old Order Amish, soon to become Conservative Mennonites. My father married a Lutheran, so I grew up in a Christian Evangelical environment. In that context, I became a "born again" Christian at age 11.

But I was 30 years old before I understood the full power God provides through His Holy Spirit. My younger brother Mark and his wife, Abby, are also "boomers" and products of the Jesus Movement. As pastors, they helped me understand the work of the Holy Spirit, which has been an important part of my life and service in Israel ever since.

By 1979 I had moved on from my job at Goodyear in Canada and had my own insurance business. I was a bachelor making lots of money and had every opportunity to do just as I thought God directed. I put my insurance business in trust with a colleague and headed to Jerusalem to study at the Institute of Holy Land Studies (now Jerusalem University

College). I didn't know anyone there—I just answered the call of God to learn more about Israel and the Jewish people.

In the *sherut* (shared taxi) from the airport on the way to Jerusalem, an Orthodox Jew in the car heard me speak in English. He responded in English, asking who I was and where I was going. When I told him, he looked stunned. A Christian who wanted to learn more about Israel and the Jewish people? How could that be?

"Where will you stay?" he asked. When I replied that I was hoping to get a room at the YMCA, he said, "No! You must stay with my family and me on your first night in Israel!" So I spent that night on their closed-in balcony. The next day, he, an Orthodox Jew, drove me, a Christian, to the Institute of Holy Land Studies on Mount Zion.

STAYING IN JERUSALEM FOR HIS PURPOSES

My graduate-level courses were intense and included subjects like Islam, historical geography, and archaeology. But the course that has served me most until today was "Physical Settings of the Bible and Ancient Related Texts," which included field trips to the places we studied in class.

At the end of the year, I had every intention of returning to Toronto, resuming my business, making lots of money, and living happily ever after.

But God had other plans!

Just as He "spoke" to me about *coming* to Israel, He now "spoke" to me about *staying.*

I had no visa, no more savings to live on, no place to live, and no real reason to be in Israel—except that I believed God told me to stay. I knew that if I had *really* heard from God, I had no choice but to obey. So in faith, I sold my business and stayed in Israel.

And as soon as I stepped out in faith, God put the pieces in place.

Dr. George Giacumakis, the director of the Institute where I was studying, said I could sleep in the room where they stored ancient potsherds and eat at the Institute. I renewed my visa and remained in the Land to discover God's purpose for me to be there.

THE BIRTH OF AN EMBASSY

In 1980 Israel passed the Jerusalem Law, which declared Jerusalem as the eternal undivided capital of Israel. The world went crazy! The 14 countries that had embassies in Jerusalem came under immense pressure from neighboring Arab oil–producing countries to not recognize this law. As a result, the embassies were all moved to Tel Aviv, and Israel was literally alone on the world stage.

However, a group of praying Christian Zionists were seeking the Lord as to what to do about the world's abandonment of Israel. Jan Willem and Widad van der Hoeven, George Giacumakis, Merv and Merla Watson, Jay and Meridel Rawlings, and a few others prayed. God was speaking to many, especially through the van der Hoevens and Watsons: this was the time for Christians to take a stand and open an international Christian embassy in Jerusalem.

George Giacumakis said, "I see preachers, musicians, and visionaries in this room, but there is not a practical one in the bunch of you. I think I know who God wants to be the practical part of this work. God told him to stay in Israel, and he did so out of obedience, not knowing why. He has all the practical background and experience needed to start such an embassy. I think he is the man. His name is Timothy King."

I was drawn into this grand vision from its embryonic beginning.

We presented a proposal for a Christian embassy to Teddy Kollek, mayor of Jerusalem; Menachem Begin, the prime minister; and Maurice Jaffe, head of the Great Synagogue. They each responded enthusiastically. Keep in mind, Israel was alone internationally, and yet here we were, a handful of Christians, representing millions of like-minded Bible-believing people around the world who stood with the Jewish State. They literally said, "Go for it!"

And we did.

I was appointed the financial director of this fledging organization despite it having absolutely no money. Johann Lückhoff was asked to be the executive director, and Jan Willem van der Hoeven, the spokesman. The Watsons became the official worship leaders.

The International Christian Embassy Jerusalem (ICEJ) was officially opened by Mayor Teddy Kollek on September 30, 1980, coinciding with another event happening at the same time: the 1980 Christian Celebration of the Feast of Tabernacles. The same group that birthed the Christian Embassy through prayer also envisioned this event, attended by approximately 1,000 people from 30 countries.

The following year, during the opening night of the 1981 Feast of Tabernacles, in what was then Israel's largest convention center, Prime Minister Menachem Begin greeted the 3,000 Christians present. But before he had even said a word, the audience rose to their feet in thunderous applause. One could see how much that reception meant to the prime minister, as Christians from around the world were *literally* standing with Israel when most of the world had abandoned her. It was at that event the phrase "Israel, you are not alone" was born.

The Christian Celebration of the Feast of Tabernacles, a project of the Christian Embassy, has become Israel's largest annual tourist event. It brings thousands of Christian pilgrims to Israel who return to their countries as true ambassadors for Israel.

ALIYAH FROM THE FORMER USSR

During the 27 years I served as the financial director of the Christian Embassy, several milestones stand out in my life of obedience, trust, and sacrifice to God's unfolding plan.

The first of these happened in the 1990s when the Iron Curtain fell and the Former Soviet Union (FSU) opened its doors, allowing Jews to make Aliyah. Jan Willem van der Hoeven, the ICEJ spokesman, announced to 3,000 Christians attending the Feast of Tabernacles that we would be chartering planes and paying for thousands of Jews to make Aliyah (return to Israel).

As I sat in the audience listening, I swallowed hard because I knew that we didn't have enough money to pay for even one plane. I prayed and prayed and prayed as I wondered, *What did he just get us into?*

As I sought God about His plan for helping Jews make Aliyah, He told me to sell seats on the planes for $500 a seat. I shared the plan with my colleagues, and we did just that. It worked! People donated millions of dollars, and to date, the ICEJ has paid for and helped more than 170,000 Jews make Aliyah!

BECOMING A FAMILY

A personal milestone also happened during this time. I had been a "confirmed bachelor," but that was about to change. In 1989 I sought the Lord for more direction, specifically for my personal life. I asked Him what He wanted from me.

His response could not have been clearer: "If you want more of me, get married!" It was that clear, that simple. I responded, "But Lord, I have failed with relationships. I have done stupid things and not done well in this area at all."

"I will be with you every step of the way," He said. Just as I had done many times before, I believed, trusted, and obeyed. I started "looking under every rock" for the woman He promised to bring.

Within months, Martha White appeared in Jerusalem, and within a few more months, we were married. Martha had been a Christian worker in Asia and the Pacific and had come to the Feast of Tabernacles. We were married January 4, 1990, in Jerusalem. Both of us were 43 years old, and in 1991, at the age of 44, God blessed us with our daughter, Anna. This old bachelor became a family man, and I have loved every minute of it.

Anna has since received a BA from Hebrew University and an MA from Tel Aviv University in Conflict Resolution. She served in the Israel Defense Forces (IDF) as a hummer tank instructor and married a Jewish believer who serves as a tank officer. They have blessed us with two granddaughters, Ella and Rotem, and we all live in one multilevel home as a typical Middle Eastern family. She and her husband continue to carry on the legacy of "blessing Israel" in their life and work.

ENDURING THE GULF WAR

In 1991 when Anna was only 3 weeks old, Saddam Hussein shot 29 Scud missiles at Israel during the Gulf War. When missiles were fired, we had to run to our sealed room, put the baby in a gas protective tent, put on our gas masks, and pray. Our prayers were answered, and we remained safe—but not without a lot of anxiety.

During that time, most Christian organizations called their people home out of harm's way. Martha's mother called her to express the opposite response. She said, "Don't you dare come home, especially now, when you must stay and support the Jewish people." Of course, we had no intention of leaving—but this was a welcomed confirmation.

When the Gulf War broke out, the leadership of the Christian Embassy was abroad on speaking tours and could not return to Israel—which meant I was suddenly in charge. So I gathered our staff of 40 and told them to pray and ask God if they should go or stay, assuring them there was no pressure either way. The next day at our staff meeting, 100 percent of the staff announced they had decided to stay.

Somehow Israeli television learned about this and wanted to interview me about it. Since I was the only one from our leadership team in Israel, Martha, our three-week-old baby, the protective gas tent, and our gas masks all appeared as guests on the TV show, *Between the Chairs*.

Because of the war, the entire nation was glued to the television as I shared what the

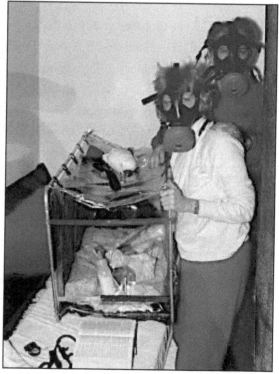

Tim and Martha with gas masks on and three-week-old Anna in a protective tent during the Gulf War, 1991

International Christian Embassy Jerusalem does and why we do it—

and that millions of like-minded Christians were standing with them during the war. I told the listeners that 100 percent of our staff chose to stay and support Israel. It was a real blessing to a hurting people—and God did it all!

ESTABLISHING AND EXPANDING THE ICEJ

The Feast and the Christian Embassy exist as an expression of love and comfort for the people of Israel. Isaiah 40:1–2 says:

Comfort, yes, comfort My people! says your God. Speak comfort to Jerusalem, and cry out to her, that her warfare is ended, that her iniquity is pardoned; for she has received from the LORD'S hand double for all her sins.

While the ICEJ headquarters was founded in Israel, branches began to open immediately all around the world. A vital branch is the USA Branch, and as the top American leader in Jerusalem, I gave special attention to its establishment. In 1986 I worked with Susan McElroy Michael to establish the USA Branch in Washington, DC. Susan then served as the USA administrator until the branch became fully operational under her leadership. Susan had been a fellow student in Jerusalem and part of the staff family since the ICEJ began. Together we organized events across the United States, and that branch provided the financial undergirding for the Jerusalem headquarters in those early years.

TRANSLATING IN ISRAEL

After stepping down from my position with the ICEJ in 2007, I determined that I had completed my life's calling and work in Israel. But once again, God had other plans. In many ways my work for the Lord was just beginning.

David Swarr and Samuel Chiang approached me in 2015 and asked me to become a founding board member of the 4.2.20 Foundation (www.4220foundation.com). I had no idea what lay ahead except that this assignment dealt with Israel's national language, Hebrew.

Some 7,000 languages exist in the world today, yet the biblical stories of Israel in the Old Testament are only available in 700. Furthermore, most Bible translations are only of the New Testament. How can Christians possibly understand the New Testament when over 24 percent of it references an Old Testament they don't even have? In response to the obvious need, the 4.2.20 Foundation created the Institute of Biblical Languages and Translation to train Bible translators in biblical Hebrew so they can translate the Old Testament.

CALLED FOR HIS PURPOSES

As a child, I learned a song in Sunday School that summarizes everything that has happened in my life over the past 43 years: "Trust and obey, for there's no other way." The thread of trust flows through all my decisions, leading to where I am today and making Israel my home.

I trusted God and obeyed His call. In return, God took this American from the "boomer" generation who knew nothing about Israel or the Jews and orchestrated a life focused on supporting His purposes for this ancient land and people.

Timothy King is the vice president of Israel operations for the 4.2.20 Foundation and vice president of administration for the University of the Holy Land. He went to Israel for the first time in 1979 to study at the Institute of Holy Land Studies in Jerusalem, then served as the founding financial director of the International Christian Embassy Jerusalem (ICEJ) for the next 27 years. He currently serves as a deacon and board member of King of Kings Congregation in Jerusalem.

Generation X

Born between 1965–1980

6

ISRAEL BECAME MY HOME

Bishop Robert Stearns

It was 1993. The Cold War was over, Bill Clinton was president of the United States, the internet was just being conceptualized, the first Beanie Babies were created, and Yitzhak Rabin was prime minister of Israel.

I was living in Jerusalem, serving several ministries—the International Christian Embassy Jerusalem (ICEJ) chief among them. I was a 24-year-old from Buffalo, New York, with a Bible college degree but virtually no context for what it meant to be residing in the Jewish State resurrected from the dustbin of history.

I was raised in the church and familiar with different streams of Christianity—from the Roman Catholicism of my beloved grandmother to the Evangelical Pentecostalism most familiar to my immediate family. I had read and memorized passages about Israel in youth group for Christmas and Easter productions and in my personal life. As a musician and vocalist, I have played and sung Davidic psalms and songs about Israel since I was young.

I didn't realize I was missing a real connection to the land of the Bible I read about all my life, but when I heard about an opportunity to volunteer at the ICEJ, I figured, why not? The idea of an adventure in the Holy Land piqued my curiosity and interest. There—in Israel as a young leader—my entire life was about to change forever.

One day wandering about Jerusalem (as I often did on international travels), taking in the sights and sounds and exploring a culture vastly different from my own, I came upon a scene in the outdoor courtyard of what I now know as the Great Synagogue.

It was an exuberant event with music and dancing, and I wanted to know what it was all about. I approached the outskirts of the crowd to engage some of the attendees in conversation. One question led to another, and the next thing I knew, I was in the middle of a celebration with a group of Orthodox Jews. They explained that today was *Yom Yerushalayim*, or "Jerusalem Day," and they were celebrating HaShem's (God's) faithfulness to the city of Jerusalem.

In that brief encounter, I had a revelation that stuck with me: these young men, with their traditional black-and-white garb and unusual customs, were praying to the same God I prayed to. The same God Jesus prayed to. The God of Abraham, Isaac, and Jacob. *My God was the God of the Jews.*

At the time, I had no framework for this new understanding. Sure, I knew the Old Testament often refers to Israel. And as someone who grew up in the church and pursued training for Christian ministry, I knew all the stories: Jonah and the "whale," Elijah and the prophets of Baal, David and Goliath.

But I, like many others, had also been taught that what *really* mattered was belief in Jesus—and that Old Testament stories only had meaning as they related to the unfolding of Jesus' birth, ministry, death, and resurrection. Furthermore, Jerusalem only had meaning in connection with the gospel being released to the world.

That life-changing encounter at the Great Synagogue in 1993 commenced a decades-long journey of discovery that continues to this day and is the focus of my life's mission: to help Christians find, love, and support Israel and the Jewish people.

A GROWING CONNECTION

During that extended trip, the Lord gave me a crystal-clear, unmistakable vision in which I saw flames of spiritual revival connecting major cities across the East Coast of the United States with the city of Jerusalem. The vision was impossible to ignore, both in its vividness and its link to my passion for revived devotion in American churches. As I inquired of spiritual leaders in my life, searching out the meaning of the vision in the weeks and years that followed, what emerged was the central importance of Israel and Jerusalem to our faith as Christians and the strategic unfolding of God's plan to unite the body of Christ in this generation. This understanding resulted in the birth of Eagles' Wings as a ministry and a growing connection to the people and Land of Israel.

As a traveler and bridge-builder by nature, I began bringing people to Israel so they could learn more about what God was doing in the Land. We participated in the annual Feast of Tabernacles celebration sponsored by the ICEJ and other conferences and gatherings. We were all hooked, as we felt like we stepped into the unfolding pages of history every time we set foot in

Robert Stearns praying at the Western Wall in Jerusalem, 2002

the Holy Land. Eagles' Wings became known for the "Israel piece" we brought to everything we did globally—my passport has been stamped at the Tel Aviv airport more times than I can count.

CHRISTIANS AWAKENING

In the early 1990s Christian support of Israel existed but was nowhere near what it is today, an organized global movement. The ICEJ's leadership spearheading the yearly Christian celebration of the Feast of Tabernacles was key to this development. Through my involvement as staff for that event, I got to know leaders from around the world who were also experiencing a transformation concerning the centrality of Israel.

In 2002, through a sequence of divinely orchestrated events, the Lord led me and the late Dr. Jack Hayford—my friend and mentor—to launch a new annual holiday on the Christian calendar in the season of Yom Kippur. At a meeting in the Consulate of Israel in New York City with a handful of Christian leaders and representatives from the State of Israel, the Day of Prayer for the Peace of Jerusalem was born. It takes place on the first Sunday of every October in over 175 nations around the world. As far as we know, it is the single largest Jerusalem-focused Christian prayer movement in history, with millions of Christians participating annually.

It was a miracle to be sure for Jews and Christians to begin relating to each other after almost 2,000 years of separation. I remember meeting significant Jewish religious and political leaders and the guarded nature of those early interactions—both sides were trying to discover if the other had a hidden agenda. But by taking baby steps toward each other, we found imperfect yet firm footholds to begin to bridge the gap.

In this new atmosphere of Jewish-Christian cooperation, the late Russian-Israeli MK Yuri Shtern cast a vision for a caucus of official dialogue between our two faith communities within the Israeli Knesset. I was privileged to be involved as these foundations were laid. As a result, the Knesset Christian Allies Caucus was launched in 2004 and continues to this day.

THE NEXT GENERATION

As these unprecedented relationships between Christian and Jewish communities grew, it became evident that no matter how historic and significant these new interactions were, they wouldn't last if we didn't involve the next generation.

So we launched a program for Christian student leaders—the Israel Experience—in which they would learn about Israel's culture, biblical and historical significance, and global impact through an immersion experience in the Land. To date, we have taken students to Israel from over 110 American universities. One of my cherished personal mementos is a handwritten letter from Nobel Prize winner Professor Elie Wiesel, recommending his students for our program.

This effort was an uphill battle from the start—so much was being taught in Western universities that cast Israel in an unfavorable light and blamed the Jewish State for terrorists' agendas against Israel's borders and her people. But the impact personal experience had on the lives of those who went to the Land was more powerful than the propaganda. Classroom knowledge could not substitute for the firsthand understanding that came from these travels, and no amount of academic demonization of Israel could steal the living revelation those young adults gained from visiting the Land.

DAVID NEKRUTMAN

One Jewish friend who became like a brother early in this journey is David Nekrutman. I met David when he worked in the office for interreligious affairs at the Consulate of Israel in New York. Several years after leaving the consulate, he became the executive director at the Center for Jewish-Christian Understanding and Cooperation (CJCUC) in Efrat, Israel, under the oversight of Rabbi Shlomo Riskin. David has been an important advisor in many of our initiatives, such as the Day of Prayer for the Peace of Jerusalem, the Israel Experience, and the Watchmen on the Wall Program—our "Israel 101" training program for Christians of all ages.

As David and I got to know each other, we realized that we shared many of the same values and goals, even though we approached issues from two very different perspectives. Over the years, we have developed a friendship and bond that goes much deeper than collaboration. Our relationship speaks to the unifying nature of God's covenant that has never changed, despite centuries of Christian antisemitism, mistrust, suspicion, and alienation from our Jewish brethren.

Even as David and I waded into unfamiliar waters relationally, it felt more like a "coming home" than entering foreign territory. It was historic.

We were onto something.

DISENGAGEMENT AND DEEPER ENGAGEMENT

In 2005 I was invited to a private meeting with Prime Minister Ariel Sharon. A few weeks later, he led the heartbreaking and controversial disengagement from Gaza. I remember awaiting the news with concern and foreboding over what would happen when Jewish families would be forced to leave their homes and farms they had tended for decades—all in the hopes of an elusive peace even the Oslo Accords and future efforts could not achieve.

As we watched the disengagement in Israel, we decided to get Christians even more engaged with this amazing land. We started outreaches to enable senior pastors (and their associate pastors, many of whom are millennials) to travel to Israel for the first time. In more cases than I can count, these pilgrimages provided a life-altering, personal, ministry-defining moment that impacted participants in a visceral way that left them undone.

Our yearly trips to Israel during the fall feasts became a highlight not only for the thousands of Christians we have taken to Israel through the years but also for my own family. My three sons have been to Israel more times while growing up than most ministry leaders or Silicon Valley business executives achieve in their lifetime!

ISRAEL IS FAMILY

As a result of our frequent visits, Israel has truly become family for my family. Our chief Israeli tour guide, the wonderful Shlomo Eyal, his wife, Tzila, and their amazing children, Aviv, Adi, and Yakir, are the closest of family to us. Something indescribable happens when Jewish and Christian families come together around Torah and the biblical feasts—it cannot be compared with any other experience this side of heaven.

We have found in the God of Israel and in each other the strength to persevere in a world violently opposed to the divine testimony the Land and people of Israel faithfully declare with their lives. It is a hope (expressed in Israel's anthem, "HaTikvah"[7]) that cannot be silenced by the threats and intimidations of a world opposed to the God of covenant.

LIFELINE AMID TERRORISM

The violence Israelis face time and again is not only directed at them. Christians in cities like Bethlehem are also increasingly subject to violent outbreaks from their Arab neighbors solely because of their faith.

When I first traveled to Bethlehem, I was shocked by the stark difference between the areas governed by Israelis (including Arab villages) and those like Bethlehem, controlled by Palestinians. The tension in the city of our Savior's birth is palpable, the air thick with an oppressive weight.

I learned that it wasn't always this way. When the Palestinian Authority was given control of Bethlehem in 1995, violence and unrest intensified, causing Christians to flee en masse. By the time the second intifada broke out in 2000, Bethlehem and the West Bank had become one of the most dangerous areas in the Middle East regarding terrorism. This reality prompted Israel to construct a security fence to

---

[7] Israel's national anthem. *HaTikvah* means "The Hope"; the lyrics are about the Jewish people's undying hope, despite centuries of exile, to return to the land promised to them through their forefathers Abraham, Isaac, and Jacob.

protect its people from suicide bombers who attempted to enter Israeli territory.

The so-called "Christian exodus" from the Middle East was personified by the alarming downturn in the Christian population of Bethlehem, especially in the years following 1995. So I decided early on that it was critically important for Christian travelers to not only visit holy sites in Israel but also meet their brothers and sisters in Bethlehem—a people struggling to survive—to show our support for their businesses and efforts in the region. This precious community of believers needs our continued heartfelt and tangible support; it is a lifeline for them.

TIME FOR JERUSALEM

When a billionaire businessman named Donald Trump was elected president in 2016, no one *really* knew what it would mean for American domestic and foreign policies. However, it quickly became evident that whatever people thought of him, this president's administration would prove to be one of the most openly supportive of Israel since the rebirth of the Jewish State in 1948.

Like many Evangelicals, I was cautiously optimistic when the proposal to move the US Embassy from Tel Aviv to Jerusalem finally went public. The move of the embassy—already enacted into law through the Jerusalem Embassy Act of 1995—had been delayed repeatedly by successive US administrations until it seemed it might never happen. But now, during the Trump administration, it was time for Jerusalem.

A year before President Trump officially recognized Jerusalem as the capital of Israel on December 6, 2017, ordering the move of the embassy, I was asked to write an online opinion piece in the *New York Times* (alongside opposing views by others) in favor of the administration's intent. I wrote that the Middle East needed principled leadership that didn't cower to fear and that the move of the embassy was an overdue action that would benefit Israelis and Palestinians alike.

The backlash I received online was intense. And on a wider scale throughout the nation, threats abounded that World War III would result if the United States made the move—that the Middle East would plunge into a bloodbath from which it might never recover. But through the great work of US Ambassador to Israel David Friedman, plans were made to move the embassy on May 14, 2018, in honor of Israel's seventieth anniversary. May 2018 arrived—and the United States delivered on its promise.

And just the opposite happened from what detractors predicted! The move of the embassy happened peacefully, and historic peace agreements followed between Israel and several Arab nations through the Abraham Accords.

As a ministry, we recognized the significance of the moment and decided these historical times called for large numbers of Christians to come to Jerusalem. So we launched the first Awake Jerusalem 72-hour worship gathering that fall in conjunction with the annual Day of Prayer for the Peace of Jerusalem. Hundreds joined for a moment that felt like it was right out of the pages of the Bible. It was the culmination and fulfillment of what many Christians and Jews had worked on together for many years.

THE PRESENT AND BEYOND

The need has never been greater for Christian advocates of Jerusalem, Israel, and her people. Israel's enemies continue to surround her and threaten her existence as she faces increased challenges on multiple fronts. In addition to ongoing terrorism and the economic impact caused by COVID-19, the pandemic interrupted people's ability to travel to Israel and demonstrate support for what God is doing in this critical hour.

However, I believe the best days are ahead for Christians and Jews to come together around our shared values. I also believe that when Israel's borders reopened, it opened the floodgates for a wave of pilgrims that may exceed anything Israel has yet seen.

My prayer for that beloved land today comes from the ancient words penned by King David:

Pray for the peace of Jerusalem: "May they prosper who love you. Peace be within your walls, prosperity within your palaces." For the sake of my brethren and companions, I will now say, "Peace be within you." Because of the house of the LORD our God I will seek your good. (Psalm 122:6–9)

Bishop Robert Stearns is the founder and executive director of Eagles' Wings, a global movement of churches, ministries, and leaders. In 1993 he had a life-changing encounter at the Great Synagogue in Jerusalem that started a decades-long journey of discovery and mission to help Christians find Israel. Since 1993 he has ministered in more than 30 nations around the world with a focus on the central importance of Israel and Jerusalem to the Christian faith and the unfolding of God's plans to unite the body of Christ in this generation.

7

FROM MATH TO LIFELONG ISRAEL ADVOCACY

Shelley Neese

As a rule, junk mail should never influence a major life decision. In my case, however, one piece of junk mail changed everything.

In 1999 my college sweetheart, Brian, and I went to the Student Union on Louisiana State University's campus to check his post office box. We had spent the afternoon under the shade of one of LSU's thousand oak trees, deliberating the timeline of our next steps. He was about to finish his undergraduate degree and apply for medical school, but I still had one year left at LSU to complete my bachelor's degree. Young and in love, we did not know how much longer we could wait to get married, and we were also not keen on living apart geographically while he went to medical school.

A pamphlet for a medical school at Ben-Gurion University (BGU) was among his mail that day at the post office. Every college student is accustomed to getting promotional brochures and letters from potential graduate schools. (Personally, I relish disposing of all irrelevant envelopes in my mailbox before even opening them.) However, this pamphlet was different—it promoted a medical school in Beer Sheva,

Israel, that focused on international health. Maybe it was the glossy desert landscape that caught his attention, or perhaps the fact that the school was associated with Columbia University in New York. Either way, he applied and later flew to New York for an interview.

Brian is a military brat. He grew up as the son of a pilot, living that military lifestyle where you relocate every three years to a new American town. Some military kids graduate high school and cannot wait to settle in one place and never move again. Others, like Brian, develop a permanent sense of wanderlust. He couldn't stay in the same place for too long, and he was already getting the itch after four years in Baton Rouge. So the idea of going to medical school in an exotic place like Israel appealed to him on many levels, even if it did not appeal to me.

I am the daughter of a preacher and teacher from a small town in Louisiana. I had never moved in my entire life except to go to college. Even then, LSU was only a two-hour drive from my home. But love has a way of clouding one's vision. If going to medical school in Israel meant that we could get married sooner and live in the same city, even if that city was across the world, that seemed worth the sacrifice.

On June 10, 2000, Brian and I were married in my dad's church. Within a month we sold our cars and few possessions, put our wedding presents in storage at my parents', and flew to Israel with nothing other than what we could fit in our suitcases. LSU allowed me to finish the last year of my degree as an overseas student at BGU's main campus in Beer Sheva.

MY INTRODUCTION TO ISRAEL

To say that we knew almost nothing about Israel before moving there is an understatement. We knew less than nothing. The problem is that we thought we knew something. We were Christians with an average familiarity with the land of the Bible. In our imaginations, we were going to spend our weekends jogging around the Galilee or hiking up the Mount of Olives, all of which we assumed were unadulterated by any modernity.

Only when I was sitting at the gate in Frankfurt, Germany, for our connecting flight to Tel Aviv did I realize that I was about to become a religious minority for the first time in my life. Before boarding the flight, dozens of Orthodox Jewish men and women stood and began praying, rocking back and forth and reading from small prayer books. Small-town Louisiana life had not exposed me to Judaism. I had no context for what modern Judaism looks like in practice. This was the first moment in my Israel journey when my ignorance was made abundantly clear. There were many more of those moments.

When we arrived in Beer Sheva to start looking for an apartment, I picked up a newspaper at a gas station after seeing a headline on the cover announcing the arrival of Israeli Prime Minister Ehud Barak and Palestinian Leader Yasser Arafat to Camp David. Though I still lacked knowledge about Israel's modern history, I thought peace negotiations were a positive sign. I even emailed my parents the picture of Bill Clinton standing next to Barak and Arafat to relieve their fears about their youngest daughter's plan to live in the Middle East. When the Camp David Summit ended on July 25 without an agreement, I remained hopeful that wars in Israel were a thing of the past.

However, before Brian and I had finished our first session of Ulpan (an immersive Hebrew language training program), the country broke into chaos. The 2000 Camp David Summit had ended without a deal, and while Barak and Arafat blamed each another, the reality was that neither leader had the strength at home to deliver on an agreement. The failure of Camp David upset the silent tension in the country.

THE SECOND INTIFADA

On September 28 the Second Intifada began, although no one was calling it that yet. At first the violence centered around the Temple Mount and consisted of rock throwing and exchanges of gunfire. The media presented it as a spontaneous Palestinian uprising in response to Ariel Sharon's visit to the Temple Mount. However, we now know that Arafat had already called for an organized uprising in the heart of the Jewish State.

With official orders from Arafat, violence soon metastasized throughout the country. Suicide bombers were a pervasive threat, as they detonated on crowded buses, in bustling malls, and at Friday markets. The Israel Defense Forces (IDF) responded to the wave of terror emanating from both the West Bank and Gaza with aerial attacks, targeted assassinations of terror leaders, and IDF ground operations into organized terror cells.

The logistics of our day-to-day life changed, and keeping up with the rules was challenging. For example, our bags had to be checked by security officers to enter a grocery store or go through the university's gates. My college classes were just getting off the ground, but suddenly, several of my Israeli professors and classmates were called up to serve in their reserve units. And a significant percentage of my American classmates were called back to their home universities that were unwilling to have their study abroad students at risk.

DIGGING DEEPER

I had been a math major before switching from LSU to BGU, but my propensity for math now felt meaningless compared to the political events I was witnessing. I was only 20 years old and did not know the difference between Hamas, Fatah, Hezbollah, or Islamic Jihad. I was desperate to learn—so I added extra classes, taking every course I could about Israel's history and the modern Middle Eastern power players. Our small apartment did not have air conditioning, so I would go to the food court in the mall and read every book about Israeli-Palestinian relations I could get my hands on.

While I was learning about the politics and significant players in the conflict, Brian and I were developing deeper relationships with our Jewish neighbors and classmates. We rarely lacked an invitation to Shabbat dinner on Friday night. The political and religious conversations around those Shabbat dinner tables represented an intense learning curve. My studies to understand the darkness enveloping the country were complemented by learning about Judaism, which helped me better understand the light I felt emanating from

Israeli Jewish homes. All I had known about Judaism before coming to Israel was from the Bible. I had never even imagined the vitality of ongoing Jewish traditions and holidays or what they could teach me about my Christian faith.

As a relational southerner, I fell in love with Israelis and Judaism before I felt any affinity for the modern Jewish nation—which I was still trying to process on an academic level. That all changed on September 11, 2001. Brian and I were at the gym on campus when we started hearing news reports about a terrorist attack in New York. We went to the home of an American friend who had cable television. At that moment, seeing footage of an airplane flying into the south tower, I realized that the justification for the attack on America was rooted in the same misinformed Islamic ideology plaguing the streets of Israel; the hijackers of Flight 175 were motivated by the same thing as the suicide bomber who detonated themself in a Sbarro pizza restaurant in Jerusalem.

THE ONGOING INFLUENCE OF ANTISEMITISM

Once I completed my bachelor's degree, I enrolled in a graduate program at BGU in Middle Eastern Studies. At that point, I was beginning to get my footing concerning Israel's 50 years of history. The graduate program looked back to the Ottoman period and the British Mandate. I studied the history of antisemitism and authored papers about incidents in Jewish history like the Dreyfus Affair and Spanish Inquisition. Studying Jewish history, particularly the persecution of Jews in Christian countries, provoked a prolonged period of inner repentance and reflection. I took a Holocaust and film class where I cried almost daily for an entire semester.

While studying so much Jewish history, I could not separate the past from what my Israeli friends were enduring in the present. I began to see the connection between the incidents of antisemitism throughout the centuries and across the globe. On March 27, 2002, Brian and I attended a large Passover Seder dinner with friends from school. During a break in the communal reading of the Seder, people learned of a terrorist attack at a Seder dinner in Netanya, Israel. The family hosting our Seder was religious, which meant that technically, they were not supposed to turn on the news. But in this case, they did. We all stared at the television screen showing images of 30 dead and over a hundred injured. Somehow, the suicide bomber had made it through hotel security with a suitcase loaded with explosives. Among the victims were Holocaust Survivors and a Swedish tourist. It was the deadliest attack of the Second Intifada. Experiencing the pain of the breaking news amid the retelling of the Exodus story affirmed in my soul that something had to be done to stop the progression of evil against the Jewish people.

In response to the Passover Massacre, the Israel Defense Forces (IDF) launched Operation Defensive Shield. The IDF had not conducted such a large-scale operation inside the West Bank since 1967. The first goal of the operation was to put Arafat in lockdown at his Ramallah residence. But as a large-scale counterterrorism offensive, the IDF had a list of targets. In Bethlehem, the IDF tracked down dozens of terrorists who had managed to get inside the Church of the Nativity. They then surrounded the church, refusing to allow terrorists to abuse holy places.

For the next 38 days, I obsessed over the news. International pressure to release the terrorists mounted as the threat to the church and the monks trapped inside grew unbearable. When the crisis was resolved—peaceably, by the standard of any other Israeli-Palestinian negotiation—I was determined to find out what happened and why those negotiations seemed successful as opposed to almost everything else going on in the Middle East.

I was taking a class on conflict management at the time, and I asked my professor if he would oversee my dissertation. I wanted to write about the crisis negotiations that occurred in Bethlehem that resulted in the deportation of the terrorists and the safe release of the monks without any damage to the church. To my surprise, my professor had been part of the Israeli crisis negotiation team in Bethlehem. He wanted the story shared, so he orchestrated the interviews I needed with the major players from all sides, including IDF negotiators, the mayor of Bethlehem, Palestinian negotiators, and a British mediator.

ADVOCATING FOR PEACE

After three years in Israel, we returned to the United States, where my dissertation landed me an internship working with a think tank associated with Harvard Law School. The think tank ran a program to teach negotiation skills to Israeli and Palestinian leaders based on the models used in Harvard's business and law schools. At that time, I still believed that advocating for peace was the best way to advocate for Israel.

However, it did not take long for me to become disheartened with the process of trying to teach rational negotiation techniques to Israelis and Palestinians. The methods may have worked for managing sewage systems, electric grids, or public transportation routes but did not suffice for highly emotional and religious issues like Jerusalem and the Temple Mount.

During one of the negotiation conferences in Israel, I went with a group of Israelis and Palestinians to dinner at the American Colony

Shelley, Brian, and their four kids on the Mount of Olives overlooking the Temple Mount, 2019

Hotel in Jerusalem. Normally, participants got along well as professionals, but at this conference, I overheard an Israeli talking with a Palestinian friend about the issue of statehood. The Israeli said that if the Palestinians wanted statehood, they should declare it, and no one could stop them. That is what Israel did in 1948, and it changed the reality on the ground.

Notably, at one point in the debate, the Palestinian admitted they do not want *two* states but *only one Palestinian state*. From his perspective, the Jewish State had no right to exist. I resigned from the internship soon after that trip, certain that if my life was meant to advocate for the State of Israel, the so-called peace effort would not be the most effective means. From that point on, I purposed to advocate for the best interests of Israel unapologetically.

DISCOVERING THE WORLD OF CHRISTIAN SUPPORT FOR ISRAEL
In 2004 Brian and I moved to Northern Virginia for his family medicine residency. I needed to find a new job based on my graduate degree in Middle Eastern Studies and my one-year internship in the peace industry—which I no longer believed was the right path. Prospects seemed quite narrow. I called Jim Hutchens, the president of The Jerusalem Connection, an organization I was familiar with from their magazine.

As a result of the interview, Jim hired me as the editor for *The Jerusalem Connection* magazine, a position I held for years. During this time, I oversaw the transition from print to digital, wrote monthly pieces for the magazine, and formed relationships with Jewish and Christian thought leaders in the Zionist world in America.

Before working with The Jerusalem Connection, I had been on my own in terms of learning about Israel. I had no idea there were already many American Christians who had arrived at the same conclusions I had through their own life experiences. Engaging with those believers has been one of the greatest gifts in my adulthood.

After several years as the magazine's editor, I took on the role of vice president of The Jerusalem Connection, and when Jim retired in

2019, the board asked me to take over as president. For the last 16 years, through my various roles with The Jerusalem Connection, I have collaborated with our incredible team of volunteers and our new vice president, Amy Zewe. We focus everything we do on our mission to inform, educate, and activate support for Israel and the Jewish people.

I believe millions of Christians in America are instinctively pro-Israel. But the media and anti-Israel organizations try to undermine those instincts in the hope that Christians lack the education to push back. In my own journey, all I could do was try and keep up with what was happening in Israel in real-time and pursue an understanding of the complex history of the long Jewish story before 1948. Education, relationships, and listening to the Lord were what led me to devote my life to advocacy for Israel. I hope to do the same for others by teaching and fostering opportunities for Jewish-Christian engagement.

And yes—The Jerusalem Connection occasionally sends junk mail to Christians, hoping to turn their lives toward Israel as well!

Shelley Neese is the president of The Jerusalem Connection. She received her MA in Middle Eastern Studies from Ben-Gurion University and is currently a graduate student at The Bible Seminary studying biblical history and archaeology. Shelley is the author of the best-selling book The Copper Scroll Project and host of the weekly podcast Bible Fiber, a year-long study of the 12 Minor Prophets.

8

DUMISANI U YEHOVAH–PRAISE THE LORD!

Dumisani Washington

I am a Christian Zionist, which means I believe the Jews are God's chosen people, and the Land of Israel belongs to them. However, I also believe that Israel's right to live in peace goes well beyond scriptural interpretation and is based on moral and historical grounds.

I was born Dennis Ray Washington on February 17, 1967, in Little Rock, Arkansas, part of the segregated South. I am the youngest of seven children. We moved to California when I was about a year old, so I have no early memories of Arkansas. I legally changed my first name to Dumisani in the early 1990s to embrace my African heritage. Dumisani comes from the Zulu phrase *Dumisani u Yehovah*, which means "Praise the Lord." My dear friend and sister, Nomathemba Sithole, a South African national of the Zulu tribe, helped me choose my new name. Nomathemba is affectionately known to our family as Malume, or "Aunty."

My parents, David and Lillian Washington, were from Little Rock. They were born in the early 1940s and were part of a vibrant Black community. My mother was a seamstress from a young age. My father's father was a sharecropper, so my father grew up on a farm that grew all sorts of crops, including cotton. My father did not graduate high school, primarily because he had to run the entire farm by himself when his brother and father fell ill.

My mother often spoke about Little Rock and the life of the community she loved. We were active members of King Solomon Baptist Church, where Reverend Thomas was the pastor. My mother told me I loved music so much as a baby that I would rock and sway as the choir sang. Unfortunately for Reverend Thomas, I was not fond of preaching. Whenever he took the podium, I would cry at the top of my lungs. As a result, my mother had to take me out of the sanctuary almost every week after the music ended. Perhaps I just wanted the music to continue. Either way, Mama said I gave our pastor a complex.

My father was a gifted singer, a leader of the men's chorus, and served on the deacon board. My mother was a deaconess and worked with the youth ministry, among many other things. She graduated from the only high school for Black children in Arkansas, Scipio Africanus (S. A.) Jones High School in Little Rock. S. A. Jones High School was the pride of Arkansas. Like many Black schools during segregation, there was a deep sense of connectedness among the teachers, administrators, and students.

Throughout the history of Black people in America, education has been the primary means of freedom and upward mobility. Black students from S. A. Jones graduated and went on to become doctors, lawyers, politicians, athletes, and clergy. My uncle, Dr. Levi Adams from the class of '51, had a long and illustrious career with the medical school administration at Brown University in Rhode Island. At Brown, two awards bear my uncle's name: an undergraduate award for service in a religious organization, project, or initiative and a scholarship for African American medical students at Brown's Warren Alpert Medical School.

Though I never experienced it directly, hearing my parents describe life in Little Rock gave me a great sense of pride. From them I learned of the Little Rock Nine—nine African Americans who participated in the desegregation of Central High School in Little Rock in 1957. My parents also taught me about the internal debate over the integration of public schools. Many Black people understood this would mean the end of their beloved S. A. Jones and other Black institutions in Little Rock. Indeed, S. A. Jones closed in 1970, and the newly unemployed teachers and administrators were not allowed to work in the "integrated" schools. For this reason and more, my mother was vehemently against forced integration.

My parents did not teach us hatred and contempt for White people but did teach us what racism was so we would be prepared to face it. They taught us not to ascribe virtue or wickedness to someone based on their ethnicity because a person's character is who they *are* and is not dependent on their race. They also taught us to speak our minds and not be afraid of anyone's disapproval—a lesson they demonstrated as much as they articulated.

A FIRE IS LIT THAT CONTINUES TO GROW

Dumisani at the Western Wall, Judaism's holiest site, in Jerusalem's Old City, 2012

I read the Bible as a child and was intrigued by everything about the Israelites. Though I loved reading the Gospels and "walking with Jesus" through the Scriptures, I was drawn more to the Old Testament. I knew the stories of David and Goliath, the Patriarchs, and the Exodus by heart. As a young adult, I wanted to learn more about the Hebrew roots of my faith. I was blessed to meet Jewish musicians who introduced me to the feasts of the Lord, such as

Passover, Pentecost, and Tabernacles. They shared songs and prayers in Hebrew that began transforming my worship and songwriting.

In the mid-1990s I started researching the Jewish Diaspora[8] because I was captivated by news of Beta Israel, the Jews of Ethiopia. I began to follow current events regarding Israel and Africa and learned about the absorption process of the Ethiopian Jews. These seemingly disparate strands of my life would become woven together in the coming years.

A friend and fellow musician had a band that performed songs of Zion and music of the Jewish people. I joined the band for a series of Christians United for Israel (CUFI) events called "A Night to Honor Israel." At these events, I learned about modern Israel—its people, culture, global charitable work, breakthroughs in innovation and technology, and security concerns. I also learned of the Palestinian refugee crisis and the nature of the Arab Israeli conflict. The more I learned, the more I understood the false charges made against Zionism and the connections between the Black struggle for justice and that of the Jews.

Black American history was something I learned in my home as a child at the dining room table, in the kitchen, and in my mother's sewing room. As a young adult, I also learned of the South African fight against apartheid from Malume, who had lived it. Knowledge of the realities of *true* apartheid exposes the false accusation of Israeli apartheid. I began to understand how Israel's enemies used the historic Black struggle for justice to demonize her—and I was personally offended. But I also learned of notable Black Americans in the 1970s who were likewise offended by the false claim that Zionism is racism.

TAKING A STAND

The first time I spoke publicly about Israel was at a Sacramento City Council meeting in 2012. The leaders were considering a proposal to

---

[8]The Jewish Diaspora is the dispersion of Israelites or Jews out of their ancient ancestral homeland (the Land of Israel) and their resulting settlement in other parts of the world.

make Sacramento a sister city with Ashkelon, Israel, and they held an open hearing on the subject. I experienced my first virulently hostile, anti-Israel crowd in a packed room divided along ideological lines. I heard the false accusations of Israeli apartheid, Jim Crow racism and segregation, and the alleged genocide of the Arab Palestinians. The attacks were relentless and baseless.

When it was my turn to take the podium, I refuted the claims of Israel's racism and discrimination. I explained that while no nation is perfect, Israel was nothing like what my parents experienced in Little Rock or Malume experienced in Durban. Israel is a free, pluralistic society forced to defend herself against an untold number of enemies bent on her annihilation. Comparing the Jewish State to what my family endured was beyond egregious, and I let everyone in the chamber know I was there to defend both Israel and the distinctiveness of the African American historical experience.

I quickly learned that people who oppose Israel do not respond well to Black people defending her. I was shocked to hear the racist comments directed at me by people who were there to "combat" racism.

The combination of shamelessly abusing my people's heritage and lying about Israel, one of the most significant regional partners to many African nations, lit a fire in me that has not diminished but continues to grow.

I've spoken at many Israel events since 2012, and I have learned that when it comes to slandering the Jewish State, no people's history or legacy is off-limits. Anyone's story—no matter how sacred or painful—will be exploited to demonize the Jews and their homeland. As I came face to face with such an extraordinary amount of disinformation and anti-Israel propaganda, my advocacy for Israel had officially begun.

THE INSTITUTE FOR BLACK SOLIDARITY WITH ISRAEL

My first trip to Israel was during Hanukkah in December 2012, as part of CUFI's African American pastors' tour. At that time, the African American outreach coordinator was Dr. Michael Stevens, pastor of The

City Church of God in Christ in Charlotte, North Carolina. Though I had long wanted to go to Israel, I was unprepared for how overwhelming Jerusalem was. While at the Western Wall (Kotel), I felt burdened to work on strengthening the Africa-Israel/Black-Jewish alliance. I will never forget the sights, sounds, and aromas of my first trip to the Holy Land, though I've returned 11 times since 2012. After that first trip, I returned to California and started the Institute for Black Solidarity with Israel (IBSI) in response to what I can only explain as a divine call. My son, Joshua, serves as IBSI's executive director.

Soon after the founding of IBSI, I also began serving as the diversity outreach coordinator (DOC) for the now over 10-million-member Christians United for Israel (CUFI), a position I held from September 2014 to May 2021.

As CUFI's DOC, I sought to spread the message of solidarity with Israel throughout the multiethnic body of Christ. The church is the most ethnically diverse organism on the planet, and America is the most ethnically diverse nation. Our goal was simply to take the Christian Zionist message to what the book of Revelation calls "every tribe and tongue and people and nation" (5:9). I also had the honor of welcoming international attendees to CUFI's annual Summit in Washington, DC. Each year Africa was among the most well-represented continents.

During my first speaking tour for IBSI, during which I met diverse anti-Zionists, I would often reflect on the words of my friend, Yaffa Tegegne. Yaffa is an Ethiopian Jew and daughter of the late Baruch Tegegne, a pioneer in the movement that resulted in the return of Ethiopian Jews to Israel. As a Black Jew and vocal Zionist during her college years in Canada, Yaffa encountered antagonists who could not understand her. In a 2013 interview with IBSI, Yaffa recounted:

I studied politics at Concordia University [which had] probably one of the biggest Arab student populations in North America. In 2002–2003 [Israeli Prime Minister] Netanyahu was supposed to come, and there was a riot, and we had a huge solidarity for Palestinian rights movement, and there were terrible incidents. I used to literally argue on campus all the time, and I think I was the only Ethiopian Jew and the only Ethiopian they had ever met, and it was very difficult for them. They didn't know how to deal with it because it went fundamentally against their entire notion. [I said things] like, "Here's a contemporary story of why we still need Israel. It's not just the Holocaust. This [Jewish persecution] has been continuously happening in recent times." They would have a really hard time dealing with me because I didn't fit the mold of their argument.

My experience was like Yaffa's. For many anti-Zionists, a Black person standing with Israel is offensive. They are unaware of—or don't care about—the long tradition of Black-Jewish cooperation in this nation. As a result, many falsehoods and deceptions have been promoted. It has become quite common to meet Black people, especially on college campuses, with a negative view of Israel, if not Jews in general. Jamie Kirchick noted in his 2018 commentary article "The Rise of Black Anti-Semitism":

Attitudinal surveys conducted by the ADL [Anti-Defamation League] consistently show that African Americans harbor "anti-Semitic proclivities" at a rate significantly higher than the general population (23 percent and 14 percent respectively in 2016).

In the 1960s Dr. Martin Luther King, Jr. well understood the factors adversely affecting the Black-Jewish relationship and the antisemitism fomenting in some circles. In a chapter in his 1967 book *Where Do We Go from Here: Chaos or Community?* (titled "Where Are We Going?"), he offered a partial explanation:

Negroes nurture a persistent myth that the Jews of America attained social mobility and status solely because they had money.

It is unwise to ignore the error for many reasons. In a negative sense, it encourages antisemitism and overestimates money as a value. In a positive sense, the whole truth reveals a valuable lesson: Jews progressed because they possessed a tradition of education combined with social and political action.

Some of Dr. King's most impassioned pleas for continued Black-Jewish cooperation came toward the end of his life. This was also when Israel's enemies were attempting to drive a wedge between Blacks and Jews and between Israel and the African nations, despite Black Americans' long history of shared struggle with the Jewish people. Mark Twain once said, "History doesn't repeat itself, but it does rhyme." I believe we are living in a time not unlike the late 1960s and 1970s, and Christians are being called to stand with—and be a blessing to—Israel and the Jewish people.

The issue of Black civil rights took center stage once again with the 2020 killings of George Floyd, Breonna Taylor, Ahmaud Arbery, and others. Israel's enemies use those tragedies and other challenges within the Black community to manipulate people into blaming and hating Israel and the Jews. Given the power of social media and the systemic way Israel and Jews are characterized on many college campuses, it can be argued that the exploitation of the Black community for the sake of promoting antisemitism is worse now than it was in the 1960s.

I explain the deeper purpose of this exploitation of the Black community in my article "What the Pro-Israel Community Got (and Still Gets) Very Wrong about Black Lives Matter." In short, Black Christians will be pivotal in this renewed fight for the direction of our community, the church in general, and our country.

RAISING UP AN ARMY

This June, my wife Valerie and I will have been married for 35 years. Our six children are ages 33 to 22, so we have been a large family for over two decades. We also have a son-in-law, a daughter-in-law, and three grandsons. By God's grace, each of our children is a supporter of

Israel and a friend of the Jewish community. Several serve on staff at IBSI or are contracted personnel with expertise in graphics, video, music production, and journalism. Our daughter-in-law, Olga, is the daughter of South African Parliament member and Israel advocate Rev. Dr. Kenneth Meshoe. Olga serves on IBSI's board of directors. We are doubly blessed that we have never had to force any of our children's involvement with IBSI. They give their time and talents—above and beyond—because the cause is important to them.

I am humbled to be able to do the work of strengthening the Black-Jewish, Africa-Israel alliance. I am also extremely optimistic about the future. As Dr. King said, "We've got some difficult days ahead, but we will reach the promised land."

To my fellows in the church, I say that we will see God move on behalf of those who stand with His firstborn—the Jewish people.

Dumisani Washington is the founder and CEO of the Institute for Black Solidarity with Israel (IBSI) and the former diversity outreach coordinator for Christians United for Israel (CUFI). He is a pastor, graduate of the San Francisco Conservatory of Music, professional musician, and author. His latest book is Zionism and the Black Church: Why Standing with Israel Will Be a Defining Issue for Christians of Color in the 21st Century *(now in its second edition). An original version of Dumisani's story was first published as an article in the* Journal of Free Black Thought:

www.freeblackthought.substack.com/p/zionism-and-the-black-church

Millennials

Born between 1981–1996

9

THE PLACE GOD CALLED ME TO

Jordanna McMillan

"I am a Zionist," I proudly told my friend as we stood in line in our second-grade classroom.

"What's a Zionist?" she asked.

"I believe God gave the Land of Israel to the Jewish people," I replied.

"I believe that!" she said.

"Well, then you are a Zionist too," I concluded triumphantly, proud to add another to the ranks.

It's my first memory of advocating for the Jewish State. I don't remember when I first started wearing a Magen David necklace—the star of David—but throughout my school years, I was rarely without it.

I grew up in a pro-Israel home and church. My parents visited Israel in 1979 and 1980 with our church, Mt. Paran Church of God, in Atlanta, Georgia. Their pilgrimage to the Holy Land not only shaped my childhood but had a future impact on my own journey to Israel. I grew up hearing their stories of the country, their beloved tour guide, being baptized in the Jordan river, walking the old Jericho Road, and hiking up Masada as Israel Defense

Forces (IDF) soldiers in front of them sang "Hinei Ma Tov."[9] I remember pouring over aged photographs from the early 80s that were so ingrained in my mind that when I first visited in 2006, I was naively surprised at how much Israel had changed.

Supporting Israel was part of the fabric of my childhood. As an 11-year-old, I attended a Christian summer camp run by Dr. Mark Rutland. It was during a chapel service at that camp that I felt I received a lifetime call from God to the nation of Israel.

MY FIRST TRIP "HOME"

From the summer I first felt the call of God on my life, I started saving money for my inaugural trip to Israel. By the time I went in 2004, I had saved enough to pay for the entire tour portion of the trip—$850. I found the trip I wanted to go on from browsing online after coming across an organization called the International Christian Embassy Jerusalem (ICEJ). Their young adult program was hosting a tour for Christians from all over the world during the Feast of Tabernacles.

I asked my mom if I could go, and her one condition was, "Only if your sister goes too." So that October, my older sister, Bethany, and I headed to Israel for 10 days of a lifetime. With kids of my own now, I am amazed at my mother's faith that enabled her to send her two oldest daughters—18 and 20 years old—overseas to what others perceived as a war-torn country.

Every trip to Israel has its memorable moments, and ours started before we ever stepped foot in the country. As two young ladies flying through Paris, we obviously fit a "profile," and because of this, we had our first experience with El Al security.

"Where did you find out about this tour?" they asked.

"Online." Security was not impressed with that answer.

"Do you personally know the people leading the tour?"

"No."

"Have you ever met them?

---

[9] A popular hymn for Israeli folk dances also sung by Israeli school children and Jewish and Israeli scouting groups.

"No."

We were taken into the bowels of the Charles de Gaulle Airport to a room with a lone, naked lightbulb hanging from the ceiling. When finally released, we were personally escorted to the front of the line to board the plane. Unfortunately, upon arriving at Ben Gurion, we learned that our bags had been "lost," and because of the delay caused by trying to find them, we missed our ride from the airport.

Despite our eventful arrival, I'll never forget the moment I stepped foot off the plane onto the tarmac at the old Ben Gurion terminal and saw the iconic "Welcome to Israel" sign above the airport doors. An incredible feeling swept over me; I felt like I was home.

Our trip was a whirlwind as we toured the Galilee, rode camels in the Judean desert, hiked up Masada, and floated in the Dead Sea. Our bus then climbed the hill from the Dead Sea to Jerusalem, and as we crested the top of the hill, there she sat like a jewel glittering on the hillside: the city of gold with the famous Dome of the Rock reflecting the setting sun.

In Jerusalem we toured the ancient sites and attended the ICEJ's Feast of Tabernacles evening sessions, where thousands of Christians from 90 nations gathered. We paraded through the streets of Jerusalem in the Jerusalem March, and I heard Israelis repeatedly shout out, "Thank you for coming to Israel!"

GOD PAVED THE WAY

When I first learned about the ICEJ tour, my mom mentioned that the organization sounded familiar, but she couldn't quite place it. While my sister and I were on the trip, she cleaned out the basement and found an old letter from 1980. When she had toured Israel with our church that year, a representative from the ICEJ met with her tour group to gather seed money to start the organization that exists today. She had donated, along with many others, to help start the organization, and while we were in Israel with the ICEJ, she uncovered the thank-you letter for her gift from all those years before. God had been paving the way.

As our first trip ended, I was already planning how I could come back. Liesl Maas, who founded and ran the young adult movement at the ICEJ, thankfully agreed to let us return and help prepare for their summer tour the following year. So following my graduation from high school, my older sister and I returned to Israel and experienced living in Jerusalem firsthand while we volunteered with the young adults' summer tour of 2005. That summer, I met a young Australian man named Shannon, who headed the ICEJ's IT department.

Summer ended, and I returned to the States to start college at Southeastern University. I began planning my class schedule with the intention of returning to Israel as quickly as possible and devised an entire plan to study abroad at Hebrew University. During this time, I also started dating Shannon long-distance, and the following summer, I returned to Israel.

LIFE-CHANGING, MEMORABLE MOMENTS

I have no idea what most young adults do during their summers, but for several years, I spent mine in Israel. Hoping to stay in the country for as long as possible after the 2006 ICEJ summer tour, I volunteered for a month at

Bethany (second from left) and Jordanna (third from right) on their first trip to Israel, 2004

INTRA: the Israel National Therapeutic Riding Association, located (at the time) on the shores of the Mediterranean Sea. That summer, I learned my first few words of Hebrew—but my stay was memorable for another reason; while I was there, the Second Lebanese War broke out.

I watched in shock as the BBC and Sky News reported on how the IDF sent a "barrage of fire" into Lebanon, leaving out the fact that Israel was aiming at military targets being used to attack Israel. The media only passingly reported on the many rockets landing in the north of Israel, fired from Lebanon and targeting civilians. We were not much of a target where we were in Beit Yanai, with Hadera to our north and Netanya to our south. But I'll never forget wondering before falling asleep at night, *What if a rocket headed for Tel Aviv falls short?* It was a small taste of what Israelis around Gaza and in other parts of the country live through regularly.

That summer held another life-changing, memorable moment. Shannon proposed to me in Jerusalem on the balcony of St. Andrew's Church overlooking the Old City. He had wanted to propose in the Galilee, but *Katyusha* rockets[10] were falling in that area.

Southeastern University approved my creative study abroad plan. Shannon and I enjoyed our wedding and then moved to Israel. I studied at Hebrew University while beginning work at the ICEJ. For the almost two incredible years I lived in Israel, I helped share the Land with as many young adults as would come on tour.

During those tours, we volunteered at IDF army bases, held outreach programs to Israeli Arab youth, helped Sudanese refugees as they flooded across the border, cleaned up parks and playgrounds, listened to survivors of intifada terrorist attacks tell their stories, cleaned elderly people's homes, organized a day camp for at-risk youth, worked in soup kitchens, and helped Holocaust Survivors. In addition, I wrote news articles and scriptural devotionals for our monthly magazine that reached hundreds worldwide and compiled a tour book containing educational materials about Israel's history and the threats she currently faced.

---

[10] *Katyusha* rockets are rocket artillery built by the Former Soviet Union (FSU) in World War II.

DC – THE SECOND-BEST PLACE FOR AN ISRAEL ADVOCATE

By August 2009, Shannon's five-year volunteer visa was coming to an end. We knew his visa would probably not be renewed but had hoped otherwise. As we packed up our home, we were heartbroken. We arrived back in America at the height of the recession. I sent my resume to every Jewish or Israel-related organization I could find in the Atlanta area, but no one was hiring.

A friend gave Shannon a job in Charlotte, North Carolina. In time, I secured a position at the Billy Graham Evangelistic Association (BGEA), where my overseas experience landed me in the international department. Part of my role was to organize the participation of pastors from surrounding countries to come and observe a nationwide outreach we were holding in Malawi. It was this experience that, months later, would make me an attractive candidate for a new organization opening in Washington, DC.

From the time we knew we had to leave Israel, moving to DC was our goal. Having lived in Jerusalem, it was "all downhill from here," but I felt that DC was the second-best place in the world for a young Israel advocate to be. Then, in 2011, Susan Michael, the ICEJ USA director, told us about a new organization started by Rabbi Benny Elon that was opening an office there.

A copy of Rabbi Elon's book *God's Covenant with Israel* had been on my bookshelf throughout college. Because I had researched every Israel organization in the DC area, I knew about the International Israel Allies Caucus Foundation and that then-Congressman Mike Pence was the cochair of the Congressional Israel Allies Caucus in the House of Representatives.

Susan put in a good word for me, and a few weeks later, I was in DC, interviewing for a position with the Israel Allies Foundation (IAF). As I walked out of the office, I knew God was opening a door for me, and a few days later, I was offered the job as their outreach coordinator.

The roots of the IAF go back to 2004 with the establishment of the Knesset Christian Allies Caucus in Israel's parliament. We take for granted the warm Jewish-Christian relations we share now, but this caucus was groundbreaking and a historic development. As the intifada raged on, tourism to Israel plummeted. Because it is such a major industry, it caused economic repercussions throughout the country. Many groups stopped going altogether, but Evangelical Christians kept visiting. Due to this outpouring of support from Christians during one of Israel's darkest times, the Israeli Knesset launched this caucus to officially reach out to Christian leaders and legislators worldwide to further Jewish-Christian relations and encourage their support for Israel.

In 2006 a sister caucus was established in the US House of Representatives to support Israel. The work began to gain momentum as more and more pro-Israel caucuses sprang up in parliaments all over the world, led by legislators of faith. In 2007 the IAF was created to coordinate the work of this growing network. Today, 50 caucuses exist in parliaments all over the world. At the Foundation, we call what we do "faith-based diplomacy." We aim to enable the men and women we work with to turn their deeply held faith into history-changing action.

Since I began at the IAF, I have planned countless events that brought pro-Israel Christian and Jewish advocates to "the Hill." In our first year we took up the issue of a united Jerusalem and the move of the US Embassy to Jerusalem. In 2011 we hosted our first commemoration of Jerusalem Day together with the Congressional Israel Allies Caucus on Capitol Hill. I met with Christian and Jewish leaders from a host of organizations to form partnerships and advocate for the issue.

By 2014 we launched "The Jerusalem Call," a movement encouraging Americans to not only pray for the peace of Jerusalem but become politically active and keep the issue on "the political frontline." Jerusalem would then become a campaign issue for President Trump, culminating in the move of the US Embassy to Jerusalem in 2018. That year pro-Israel Christians from across the country gathered in DC for the ICEJ's American Christian Leaders for Israel (ACLI) conference. While many of our IAF staff attended the embassy's opening in Jerusalem, ACLI and the IAF held the largest celebration outside of Jerusalem in Washington, DC. The second day of the conference—eight months pregnant with Shannon's and my second baby—I emceed an IAF Jerusalem Day event. It was an incredibly joyous occasion, the culmination of years of hard work to protect the future of Jerusalem.

From hosting Jerusalem Day events on Capitol Hill and for student groups from the United States and abroad to speaking at international conferences and AGLOW groups visiting DC, I treasure every moment I can speak and share about this amazing nation. Through my work at the IAF, I have also been privileged to be a board member of the Hidden Light Institute, which directed and released a film on the life of former Israeli Prime Minister Menachem Begin.

But in all that I have done, my favorite work has been taking legislators to Israel. I have planned, led, and been a part of US state legislator, US congressional, and international parliamentarian tours to the Land for 11 years. We take our delegations into the biblical heartland—the land Jordan named "the West Bank" but whose biblical and historical name is Judea and Samaria. A decade ago, it was rarely visited by many in Washington because it is a complicated region. However, it is brimming with rich biblical history, incredible people, and a glorious future for those who call it home.

THE PLACE I ENCOUNTER GOD

While advocating for Israel and standing with the Jewish people is my calling, Israel has always been and continues to be a place I encounter the God of Israel. One stormy evening in 2016, we brought a group of Texas state legislators to Shiloh in Samaria. As the legislators watched a film on biblical Shiloh and the modern excavations there, I stole away to pray at this amazing biblical site where Hannah petitioned God for a baby all those years ago. There I prayed for a dear friend and fellow Israel lover who had just lost her baby—and then asked the Lord to bless Shannon and me with another baby. A year and a half later, the answer to that prayer was our darling daughter, who we named Shiloh.

It is not just the work that has brought deep satisfaction and a sense of fulfillment but the people I have been privileged to work with along the way: Susan Michael (who has been a mentor and dear friend), the great and humble Rabbi Benny Elon (z"l), Daniel Williams, Joseph Sabag, Josh

Reinstein, Leopoldo Martinez, Bram and Liesl Maas, the ladies of the AGLOW ministry who have prayed with me for Israel and prayed me through many hard times—and countless others. I could not have done it without the support of my husband Shannon and our three blessings from the Lord, Boaz, Shiloh, and Yael, who always travel with us to the Land.

I love Israel's amazing past, where you walk in the footsteps of the people in the Bible. I love its present and how Israel makes the Middle East—and the entire world—a better place. It is a blessing to the nations, as God said it would be, through its many contributions to medicine, the sciences, technology, security, agriculture—the list goes on. The modern reestablishment of the nation of Israel is a testament to the faithfulness of God.

One of my favorite quotes is attributed to the author and theologian Frederick Buechner: "The place God calls you to is the place where your deep gladness and the world's deep hunger meet." The world needs more men and women who will fight against the rising tide of antisemitism and stand with the Jewish people and the State of Israel, and it is my deepest joy to do so.

Jordanna McMillan serves as the outreach and communications director for the Israel Allies Foundation in their Washington, DC, office. From speaking at international pro-Israel conferences to leading US congressional and state legislator trips, Jordanna is passionate about educating leaders and mobilizing them to support Israel. She lives with her husband and three children in the Washington, DC, area.

10

LEADING A NEW GENERATION

Jesse Rojo

Merriam-Webster Dictionary describes providence as "divine guidance or care." *Lexham Bible Dictionary* defines it as "God's plan and interaction with His creation." According to the Bible, God has revealed Himself to men—and His purposes for humanity, which He has chosen to accomplish through Israel. In His providence (divine guidance), God guides history in its intended course and calls us to play a pivotal role in His ultimate plan for humanity.

Providence is the best word to describe how I came to care about educating others about ancient and modern Israel and standing in solidarity with the Jewish people. Before my role as director of Philos Latino at The Philos Project, I knew nothing about the Israeli-Palestinian conflict or the history of antisemitism and little about today's cultural battle surrounding modern Israel.

Yet when I was asked to come to work with Philos in US Hispanic communities, as sure as I was sitting on that church pew that Sunday afternoon, I was sure I had to say yes—I knew providence had led me to this moment.

A CHILDHOOD CURIOSITY ABOUT THE JEWISH PEOPLE

I was born and raised in Washington Heights, upper Manhattan, New York, to Dominican immigrant parents. Growing up in The Heights, as we called it, was a wonderful childhood experience in the 1990s and early 2000s.

I recall summers filled with hundreds of Spanglish-speaking children running through open fire hydrants and playing water wars and manhunt at night. The fall often burst with traditional Caribbean folk music, family feasts, and enthusiastic baseball gatherings in the park. During the winter holidays thousands of illuminated fire escapes would light up the city nights. The Heights—like Lin-Manuel Miranda's Tony award-winning musical and movie adaptation of *In the Heights* depicted—was our little Dominican Republic.

But Washington Heights is a more diverse community than a Broadway musical portrays. The Jewish presence in Washington Heights dates to the Revolutionary War. Yeshiva University—one of the world's premier Jewish institutions—relocated to The Heights from its original location in the Lower East Side by 1929, making the neighborhood's Jewish community even more prominent. By the 1930s, before Washington Heights became our little Dominican Republic, it was the Jewish people's Frankfurt on the Hudson because of the thousands of German Jews who fled Nazi Germany.

The Heights has always been home to many immigrant communities. As a young Dominican boy, one of my favorite pastimes was buying Marino's Italian ices from the corner bodega while listening to live Irish bagpipes being played in the park. However, while many immigrant communities moved on, the Jewish community stayed. As Dominican US Congressman Adriano Espaillat pointed out at The Philos Project's Sixth Annual Jewish-Latino art exhibit "Nosotros" ("Us") hosted at Yeshiva University:

Even during the tough times when the name [Washington Heights] was synonymous with crack, drugs, and murder, the

106

Jewish community remained and worked with those of us who stayed to make this a stronger neighborhood.

Unfortunately, I didn't experience the era Rep. Espaillat described. In my childhood, I had few interactions with Jews, and I always wondered why—especially considering how much I learned about Israel and the Jewish people at church every weekend.

I was also aware of the common past Jews and Latinos share, one dating to the discovery of the New World. When Christopher Columbus began his first transatlantic voyage on August 3, 1492, it is believed he was accompanied by a considerable number of Jews fleeing Spain to escape antisemitic measures imposed by the monarchy.

And yet I knew so little about my Jewish neighbors who lived right across the street. That curiosity remained with me for years. And I wondered whether the God of Israel in the Bible was still the God of the Jewish people today.

A RADICAL REVELATION ABOUT GOD'S COVENANT WITH ISRAEL TODAY

Because of what I learned from the Bible about God's covenant with Israel, I did not hesitate to respond to an opportunity to meet Jewish families in Skokie, Illinois, while I attended seminary. On my way to meeting them, I prayed, "Lord, give me the chance to see you work among your people. Show me you're still with them. I've read about them in the Bible but never encountered them personally."

God answered my prayer in the most unusual way.

The outreach my seminary had planned in the Jewish neighborhood seemed like a total failure. Not one person had opened their door to us. While waiting for others to return to the bus, I went to grab a cup of coffee at the 7-Eleven. As I walked to the coffee area, a Jewish lady approached me. She asked if I could get her a coffee cup because they were out of her reach.

As I handed her the cup, her countenance dramatically changed. She suddenly began to cry hysterically, and I had no idea why. The only thing I knew to do was to pray for her. When I finished praying, her countenance changed again. Now she had a beaming smile and thanked me repeatedly as we left the store.

I never saw that lady again after that day. I returned multiple times, hoping to follow up with her, but it was as if she had never existed. No one in the neighborhood knew her. It took me years to understand what God was trying to teach me that day. I believe that radical experience was His way of showing me that He is still watching over His people and that the work of redeeming our historically broken Jewish-Christian relations will not be accomplished by human hands but by Him—in His perfect time.

AN IRRESISTIBLE CALLING TO STAND WITH ISRAEL AND THE JEWISH PEOPLE

When I started seminary, I had a simple plan: I would graduate in three years and then return to my home church in New York to help with the youth ministry. Little did I know, however, that God was about to change my journey dramatically.

Before leaving for seminary, my pastor had sternly warned me about the importance of graduating. So I was taken aback when amid my studies, he asked me to leave seminary to start working in the ministry. After seeking much council, I concluded it was unwise to abandon my studies and current ministry obligations. So I respectfully declined my pastor's request and finished my seminary degree.

After graduating, I returned to my home church because I had promised to do so. However, when I arrived that first Sunday morning, the pastor pulled me aside and informed me that I was no longer welcome there. Those words—and the fact that I was no longer welcome in the church in which I had grown up—caused one of the most painful wounds I had ever felt in my heart.

There is a popular Dominican proverb for situations like these that says, *"No hay mal que por bien no venga"* ("There is no evil that does not occur for a good purpose"). The following Sunday, I visited another church, and a new chapter in my life began.

The first person to welcome me at this new church was Robert Nicholson, the current president and founder of The Philos Project. Our first meeting occurred about a year before he launched the organization. As our friendship grew, my childhood curiosity about the Jewish people resurfaced. Robert taught me about modern Israel and his vision for The Philos Project.

The more I learned, the more I was reminded about the distressed Jewish lady with whom I had the radical encounter during my time in seminary. I asked myself if this was all part of God's providence. *Was everything good and bad that I experienced in my life culminating at this very moment?*

A year later, on a Sunday afternoon, Robert asked me to come and work with him. I knew I had to say yes, but I did not know what I was getting myself into.

MY EYE-OPENING TRIP TO ISRAEL

In 2014, two months into my new job at The Philos Project, Robert decided to take his first three founding employees on a trip to Israel. At first, I could barely contain my excitement. Growing up as a Christian, I had always longed to visit the Holy Land—to walk through the Old City and visit the places Jesus taught His disciples to pray and where He died and was resurrected. Going to Israel was a dream I had always hoped would one day come true.

As I researched about Israel, I discovered many Americans' negative reactions concerning recent conflicts between Israel and her neighbors. Sadly, I wasn't sure I still wanted to visit the Holy Land. These concerns were intensified by friends and family members who were skeptical about my safety. I was also engaged to be married, and the trip was two weeks before my wedding, which added to everyone's concern.

Nonetheless, I went on that November trip. When I first arrived in the Land, fresh off the plane at Tel Aviv's Ben Gurion Airport, I gazed over the Judean hills and valleys I had read about in the Bible. A soft and pleasant afternoon breeze, rich with a fresh Mediterranean scent, brushed across my brow as I carried my luggage through the airport to our rented SUV, which took us to our East Jerusalem hotel.

The drive to Jerusalem was peaceful and the landscape alluring, and despite my initial hesitancy about the trip, I began to be optimistic about my upcoming time in Israel. However, my sense of expectancy quickly ended as we approached the front of our hotel and were engulfed by a fog that we first assumed was smoke from burning trash. We quickly realized we were mistaken as a burning sensation seared our faces, and a thick torrent of tears and mucus flowed down our faces like angry currents after a heavy rain. This unexpected contact with tear gas made me nostalgic for my home in the United States, and I went to my room that night thinking, *What in the world have I gotten myself into?*

Jesse atop the Mount of Olives with the Temple Mount in the background on his first visit to Israel, the day after the tear gas incident, 2014

The following morning, I gazed out the window in the hallway outside my hotel room. Looking left, I saw a group of young Palestinians with scarfs over their heads angrily waving sticks and stones at the Israel Defense Forces (IDF) with whom they were trying to provoke an altercation. The IDF stood to my right, waiting for the Palestinians' next move. My window was positioned just in between the two groups, and in that moment (and for the rest of my time in the Land), I was challenged to consider what it meant to reconcile my faith concerning Israel with what was happening right before my eyes. Israel was no longer just a biblical concept but a geopolitical reality in which millions of lives are at stake.

Social philosopher Eric Hoffer once said, "It is easier to love humanity as a whole than to love one's neighbor." Part of the problem that has plagued the Israeli-Palestinian conflict is that for far too many of its advocates, the conflict is just a concept. Israelis and Palestinians are figureheads who affirm their respective ideologies. But how many advocates have stood where we stood that night in East Jerusalem? How many have sat with a local Jewish family on Shabbat or a local Palestinian at a coffee shop to listen to their stories?

A more inherent problem is how we generally perceive the Jewish people. The Philos Project commissioned a survey in 2017 with Lifeway Christian Research, in which over 1,000 US Hispanics (Catholic and Protestant) were asked basic questions concerning the Jewish people and Israel. Although a majority said they had a positive perception of the State of Israel (45 percent), a majority also had a negative perception of the Jewish people (42 percent).

At least one data point explains this apparent contradiction: over 60 percent said they had never met a Jewish person. This reality illustrates the accuracy of Eric Hoffer's analysis. To truly love a people group, we must start with individuals. And to advocate on their behalf, our advocacy must be incarnational, following the example of Jesus Christ, whom the Bible says, "became flesh [meaning, 'incarnate'] and dwelt among us" (John 1:14).

That's what The Philos Project set out to do.

A NEW ERA OF JEWISH-LATINO AND JEWISH-CHRISTIAN RELATIONS

Philos is the Greek word for "friend." Our work at Philos Latino seeks to close the gap between Jews and Latinos by creating a greater awareness of our shared values and history, promoting friendship and solidarity between our communities. Whether Latinos know it or not, the Jewish people have always lived among us. But more than just living among us, they have significantly contributed to our culture, democracy, and economic development.

Haitian-Dominican historian Jean Ghasmann Bissainthe, in a copy of his book I found in the Dominican Republic's national archive titled

Judíos en el Destino de Quisqueya[11] ("The Jews in the Destiny of Quisqueya"), claimed that Jewish communities in the Island of Curaçao (just off the coast of Venezuela) were the "cornerstone" of Dominican independence. In other words, the Dominican Republic is a democracy today in considerable measure because of Jewish support in the 1800s.

Philos Latino seeks to educate US Hispanic and Latin American communities about Jewish history through art and film. At the time of this writing, we had just hosted our sixth annual art exhibit at Yeshiva University, attended by hundreds of Latinos and Jews, government officials, and pastors. We have created several documentaries, one of which is currently circulating in film festivals around the world and has recently been nominated for an award for the eighth time.

Through this work, I have learned that the Jews are a great and unique people, and there are lessons from their history that can inspire our generation to be just as great. Ambassador Jorge García-Granados, chief of the Guatemalan delegation to the United Nations in 1947 and member of the United Nations Committee on Palestine (UNSCOP), said it best in the preface to his historical account, *The Birth of Israel*:

> I am convinced that lessons for the entire human race are to be found in the struggle of the Jews. They have proved that against all possible odds, faith in a cause, the spirit of sacrifice for an ideal, will win through. That is the lasting lesson for us all: faith is stronger than material force, and in the final battle, he conquers who fights for what he knows is just and right.[12]

For this reason I am proud to stand with Israel and the Jewish people. I firmly believe we all must be better informed about their history, culture, and identity. Being uninformed does our Jewish neighbors a disservice—depriving the entire human race of lessons that can

---

[11] *Quisqueya* (or *Kiskeya*) is one name for the Dominican Republic believed to mean "mother of all lands" in the Taino language.

[12] García-Granados, Jorge, *The Birth of Israel: The Drama as I Saw It*, 1st ed, Preface (New York: Alfred A. Knopf), 1948.

promote unity in a time of polarization and inspire hope in a time of despair.

We are living in exciting times! This is the first time in 2,000 years of church history we are witnessing a thriving Jewish nation. The reestablishment of the State of Israel is a monumental event for Christianity because it challenges historic Replacement Theology and Christian antisemitism at its core.

As I look back at how far the providence of God has brought me, I am more convinced than ever that God is raising a new generation of Christians willing to move beyond the past toward a future with our Jewish neighbors. This is indeed a unique time for Jewish-Christian relations.

As long as I have breath in my lungs, I will continue to challenge my generation to fight for what is just and right, which in our time, means standing with the State of Israel and in solidarity with the Jewish people.

Jesse Rojo is the director of Philos Latino, part of The Philos Project, a Christian leadership community that seeks to promote positive Christian engagement in the Near East. Jesse holds a BA in Theological Studies and has pioneered bilingual programs to engage and educate the Christian Hispanic community on Israel-related issues. He is the executive producer of two short films: Israel a Cappella: El Sonido de la Verdad *("The Sound of Truth") and* Cosechas de Lluvia *("Rain Harvesters"), nominated for awards eight times in film festivals around the world.*

11

IT WAS JUST THE BEGINNING

Joshua Adams

There I was—behind closed doors and crying out to the Lord in a cocktail of emotions.

After all the Lord brought me through up to that point, I was filled with questions and far from getting any answers. Why have I gained so much only to have it all taken away? Was this the beginning or the end? Where do I go from here? As I played Casting Crowns' "Praise You in This Storm" on full volume, I cried out to the Lord through wordless groans. I couldn't make sense of how I was supposed to pray or where to begin.

Ever been there before?

And that's when it happened. The music in my headphones suddenly went silent. In the middle of the night, in Jesus' boyhood town less than 100 yards away from where His mother, Mary, gathered drinking water 2,000 years ago, I had a personal encounter with the Lord unlike I had ever experienced before. What He said to me that night would stir my heart for years to come.

HOW IT ALL BEGAN

But that's not how the story begins. It started when I was a little boy growing up in the small town of DeLand, Florida. Soon after my parents introduced me to the Lord as a young child, I accepted Jesus into my heart. When I was nine years old, I became a more active follower of Christ and started to read the Bible. Though I had difficulty comprehending the Scriptures at times, my love for the Lord grew profoundly, and with it, a deep curiosity for the land of the Bible. Before I finished elementary school, I had a few life goals: to serve the Lord all my days and to see Israel at least once. So I prayed fervently from elementary school through college for one chance to see the Holy Land.

As my prayers to see the land of the Bible increased, so did my passion. My mandatory ninth-grade history paper on Harry Truman became an essay on the founding of Israel. My tenth-grade history project (for 25 percent of my class grade) was all about Israel. My first PowerPoint presentation for my eleventh-grade public speaking course focused on Israel. But through all of this, I remained unaware of the "pro-Israel movement."

Once I made it to my dream school at the University of Florida, the doors of the pro-Israel universe opened. As a sophomore, I was spread thin from managing a student-run ministry—Christian Business Leaders (CBL)—and working part-time while taking a full slate of challenging classes. Meanwhile, my younger brother, who had a knack for politics, introduced me to the pro-Israel movement through a club called Gators for Israel (GFI). Through GFI, the American Israel Public Affairs Committee (AIPAC) empowers college students to advocate for pro-Israel policies on campus and with their local members of Congress.

Just as my brother was getting involved, GFI was piloting a scholarship trip to Israel for Christian leaders through an organization called Passages. Initially, I ruled out that dream opportunity because of my busy schedule. But I soon gave in to my brother's persistence in urging me to apply for an adventure of a lifetime. Miraculously, I was chosen from a large pool of student leaders to make the pilgrimage to the Holy Land. To say I was ecstatic is an understatement.

FINALLY ON MY WAY TO ISRAEL

It was May 21, 2017, and I was on my way to Israel for 10 days! I could hardly sleep on my first-ever international flight. As we rounded out our 10-hour voyage, I was occupied with comparing the islands outside my plane window to the map of Paul's Mediterranean journey in my *Life Application Study Bible*. The morning we touched down was monumental—and it wasn't just because of my heightened realization that the land of the Bible was a real place.

Just 30 minutes before we arrived, Air Force One landed with then-President Donald Trump. It was his first international trip as president, and that week, he would become the first-ever acting US president to visit the Old City of Jerusalem. Before President Trump, many world leaders and US presidents had not recognized Jerusalem as the eternal capital of Israel. So this president's visit was a historical precursor of his decision to move the United States Embassy to Jerusalem several months later.

We spent our first day in Israel in Tel Aviv, where we toured the city and learned about the "Old New" country's rebirth. I was fascinated by the resilience of the Jewish people who withstood centuries of hardship, a Holocaust that threatened their existence, and a war against Israel on all fronts that began minutes after the modern State's founding on May 14, 1948.

As I learned how Israel overcame seemingly impossible obstacles to establish a prospering country, it became increasingly evident that the Lord has maintained His eternal covenant with Israel. As Genesis 17:7 says, "And I will establish My covenant between Me and you and your descendants after you in their generations, for an everlasting covenant, to be God to you and your descendants after you."

We spent the following few days touring the Galilee region in Nazareth and the surrounding towns on the Sea of Galilee. The area was breathtaking—especially from the top of Mount Precipice, where Jesus walked through the angry mob untouched. The top of the mountain oversees the Jezreel Valley, a valley full of biblical sites and now settlements with flourishing agriculture. Some believe it is the location where the final end-times battle will take place between the antichrist's army and the Lord Jesus Christ with His army. There I connected that although Jesus was nearly thrown off this mountain, he will return there to triumphantly save Israel and the church and begin His millennial reign over all nations of the earth.

The next few days in Galilee were full of discovery as we toured the biblical towns of Capernaum, Magdala, Tiberias, Caesarea Philippi, and many others. We had a sobering taste of reality when we saw minefields and cannons from previous Syrian offensive attacks in the same area. As we made our way north, our trip was full of discoveries. In Jish we met Aramaic Christians who have lived in the area possibly since the beginning of the church. When we arrived at the northern border, we saw an active outpost of Hezbollah, a terrorist organization seeking Israel's destruction. And as we moved toward the border with Syria, we saw a large cloud of smoke, possibly related to the ongoing Syrian Civil War—a suspicion shared by the UN guard and our tour guide.

Midway through the trip, we traveled south to see Jerusalem, the city of all cities. Our itinerary was full of incredible visits to possible locations of the crucifixion and burial of Jesus, the old City of David, the Western Wall, and many others. I fell ill for three days, but by the grace of God still managed to have an invaluable, educational time in that great city. My most memorable experience occurred on Shabbat when we danced with Israelis at the Western Wall and joined a local family for a heartwarming Shabbat dinner.

After continual prayer, my sickness and fever vanished the day after Shabbat. It was a miracle, especially considering what came next. On May 28 our group went to Yad Vashem, Israel's Holocaust Museum. It was a day that changed my life forever. Upon entering the museum, one of the first things people see is a video of Polish Jews in the 1930s dancing on Shabbat, just as I had danced with my new Jewish friends the previous night. However, the exhibits that follow quickly take a turn for the worse—horrific images of Holocaust victims, some of which are fresh in my mind to this day.

A NEW SENSE OF PURPOSE

I was shaken to the core by what the Nazis used to justify the persecution of the Jewish people to the German population. They used antisemitic quotes from Martin Luther, St. Augustine of Hippo, and other renowned church leaders to appeal to Catholics and Protestants, who made up 98 percent of Germany's population in the 1930s. I broke down in tears. It was too much to process—the horror of how millions of Christians could be complicit in the atrocious things done to Jews and other minorities. I left the museum with difficult questions and no encouraging answers, but a new sense of purpose was birthed in my heart that day.

As the trip came to an end and our bus made its way back to Ben Gurion Airport, I was deeply grateful and longing for more. While others on the bus sang their new favorite Israeli songs, I was deep in thought and prayer. At that moment, I heard the Holy Spirit mysteriously say to me, "This is just the beginning."

Unaware of the meaning of this conviction, I went on with my life and started a summer internship the following week. When I moved to Tampa to start work, a sense of discouragement overcame me, and I was unsure of what God wanted me to do with my life. On this dreary day, the Lord sent a woman named Deborah who spoke for God and proclaimed that I was "anointed to teach people of many cultures and languages, both great and small." She told me many things, including that the Lord would lead me to cross borders I didn't think possible.

Next to the words that assured me of my salvation, this was the most uplifted I had ever been because of the actions of a fellow Christian in my life. Deborah had acted in obedience to the Lord and had spoken life over me according to 1 Corinthians 14:3: "He who prophesies speaks edification and exhortation and comfort to men." I was undoubtedly being exhorted to do *something*.

BECOMING A FRIEND OF THE JEWISH PEOPLE

In the following days and weeks after returning home from work each day, I prayed fervently and looked for opportunities to do what the Lord called me to do. Within three weeks, I discovered a program through The Philos Project called the "Galilea Fellowship." The three-month endeavor was an opportunity for young people who had been to Israel to deepen their Israel experience. The activities included teaching English at local schools in the Galilee, studying Jewish-Christian relations, performing community service in the area, participating in excavations, and touring the Land. It was everything I could dream of and more. The Lord was gracious and orchestrated a way for me to go, and in the spring of 2018, I returned to Israel.

No question, it was the most exciting and adventurous 87 days of my life. I spent my time living in the Old City of Nazareth, next to two Arab Christian schools where I helped teach—on the former stomping grounds

Joshua teaching at Bet Sefer Kadoorie, an Israeli school near Mount Tabor in Northern Israel, February 2018

of a certain first-century carpenter. I taught English to hundreds of Jews, Arabs, and Bedouins ages 12 through 18. The Jewish students came from all over the world—South America, Africa, Europe, and Asia, not to mention a few non-Jewish students from East Asia. I enjoyed teaching so much that I sought out opportunities to teach outside the regular hours of the program. I found so much joy not just because of my passion for teaching but because of how warm, welcoming, and eager the students were. It was unlike anything I had ever experienced in America.

After school, our program director, Dr. Faydra Shapiro, facilitated classes on Jewish-Christian relations, contemporary Israeli society, Israel's history, and the Hebrew language. In retrospect, my experience at Yad Vashem laid the foundation for my learning experience throughout those courses. Though I'd like to say I had closure on Christian complicity leading up to the Holocaust, I left the program with even more questions than answers. But more important than receiving closure, I became an emboldened pro-Israel activist and friend of the Jewish people. Moreover, the entire experience deepened my love for the country and the people who warmly welcomed me into their homes, synagogues, and schools and invited me to Shabbat dinners.

On days off, the possibilities for adventure were limitless, and I toured Israel extensively with my new best friend and roommate, Sergio. We went to Jerusalem, Tel Aviv, Haifa, Bethlehem, and many other areas. We befriended and crossed paths with many fascinating people from Israel and all over the world, including a former advisor under Prime Minister Netanyahu, a *Forbes* 30 under 30 award recipient, famous Israeli Christian singer Elihana Elia, and President Trump's faith advisory council.

During the meeting with President Trump's faith council, I talked extensively with James Dobson, founder of Focus on the Family. While at lunch on the Sea of Galilee, he shared much wisdom with me that has benefited my walk with Christ to this day. We even exchanged letters in the months following my extended stay in Israel.

WHERE DO I GO FROM HERE?

As I neared the end of my time in Israel, I was overwhelmed with gratitude but also melancholy. After all, these had been the best three months of my life—but I wondered, *Where do I go from here?* There I was, lying on my bed in Nazareth, when the worship music on my phone abruptly paused. After a moment of silence, I heard a word from the Lord in my heart: *Be still, and know that I am God.*

I became still. It was a verse I hadn't heard or read in a few years and had almost entirely forgotten until that moment. I was blown away when I googled the rest of the verse, which says, "I will be exalted among the nations, I will be exalted in the earth!" (Psalm 46:10 NIV). I was encouraged that the Lord was with me and was reaffirming His invitation to help make His name known among the nations.

The two airplanes that carried me back to Florida from Israel were nearly full, yet I was seated next to an empty seat on both flights. These vacant seats became a cherished symbol for me that the God of Israel came home with me. I returned one more time to Israel to lead a Passages tour, which was a chance to give back to another generation of students who would have a life-altering experience in the Jewish State like me.

After graduating from college, I accepted a fundraising job at AIPAC— the same organization that invested in Gators for Israel, which introduced me to the pro-Israel movement. While at AIPAC, I met Rebeca, the love of my life. We were married—and Sergio, my former roommate, stood by my side as a groomsman.

If there is something I can share from these experiences, it is my belief that every Christian and Jew who is able should make the pilgrimage to Israel at least once in their life. Regardless of where you stand in your faith and politics, it is an experience guaranteed to bring perspective, self-discovery, and an encounter with the Creator of the universe like no other.

I don't know when I will have the opportunity to return to Israel. Still, I have dedicated myself to ensuring my family members experience the Holy Land and the miracle of the modern State of Israel. I was recently blessed to see my wife's parents make the pilgrimage, and I am currently helping plan a trip for other members of her family in 2023. I intend to take my wife and future children on their first trip to Israel.

Whatever the future may hold, I am wholeheartedly dedicated to advocating for the support of Israel within my church community and ensuring that future generations of Christians stand side by side with God's chosen people—those with whom He made an eternal covenant.

Joshua Adams is a client strategy associate at Targeted Victory. Joshua's interest in and passion for Israel began in elementary school and continued to grow through college, where he became involved in the American Israel Public Affairs Committee (AIPAC). He went on his first pilgrimage to Israel with Passages and returned to lead a subsequent tour. After graduating from college with a master's degree in international business, he worked with AIPAC.

12

FROM BUDDHA TO THE GOD OF ISRAEL

Allison Ngo Griffin

When people first meet me and ask what I do for work, I always get the same reaction: pure confusion. They look at me, a 30-year-old, 5'4" Chinese Vietnamese millennial girl from Houston, Texas, and they immediately ask, "Why do you care so much about Jerusalem and Israel?"

I grew up in a dedicated Buddhist household—so dedicated that my grandparents were formally divorced in the 90s to become monks and run a Buddhist temple in Houston. With my Buddhist background, I felt immense pressure to live a life that honored and brought glory to my family name.

When I was a young girl, my mom encountered the Holy Spirit after hearing the gospel at a funeral, and she gave her life to the Lord. Immediately my mom's new faith started causing conflicts in my family, so I began to hate this "God," this "Jesus" she was now following. Family members began to talk about divorce. One day I asked my mom, "Why are you being so disobedient? Why can't you follow Buddha like the rest of us?" She answered, "One day, you'll understand." Without ever attending a church or a small group, and while hiding her Bibles in my bathroom cabinet, she lived out her faith in secret and prayed.

I pursued a degree in biology at the University of Texas, Austin, with a full scholarship. I had the lofty dream of becoming a doctor, but during college, something stirred a desire for politics in me. As a result, I began to live a double life in which I strove to keep up with my rigorous biology course load to please my family while also becoming more politically active.

To deal with the stress of my situation, I turned to alcohol and drugs— not realizing that my choices were leading me deeper into depression, anxiety, and an eating disorder. I experienced my first panic attack in my junior year of college and woke up in a hospital. The doctors informed me that I was 88 pounds and on the verge of heart failure.

I could have turned to the Lord at this point, but instead, I turned to myself. I blamed all my problems on my parents and pursued self-love. Even though I graduated with my biology degree, I informed my parents I was dropping the medical path for one in politics. I started managing campaigns and eventually became a legislative director for a representative in the Texas House of Representatives.

On the outside, it looked like I was living my best life. But on the inside, I was crumbling. In May 2015, while working at the Texas capitol, the weight of depression and shame continued to suffocate me, and thoughts of suicide enveloped my mind. I ran to the bathroom with a bottle of pills. I started screaming to God: "If you're as real and as good as everyone says you are, reveal yourself to me—because if not, this life is not worth living!"

I met Jesus that day, and He gave me my first vision. He showed me what my life would be like if I chose to follow Him.

REPLACEMENT THEOLOGY

Brand new in my faith, I started attending a megachurch in the Dallas Fort Worth area. Despite growing up without a Christian background, I knew the importance of the Bible. When I started reading the Bible, I asked a new friend in my community group, "What does it mean when it says Israel and Judah? Is this the same Israel that I see on the news?"

I remember her response clear as day: "When the Bible refers to Israel and Judah, God is talking about the church today."

Her answer satisfied my curiosity, and from then on, I gave little thought to Israel and the Jewish people. I fully embraced the lie of Replacement Theology that says God divorced His chosen people because they

Allison in Jerusalem helping to prepare for the Jerusalem Prayer Breakfast in 2022

rejected Jesus, and we, "the church," are His new bride. And as His new bride, we will now receive all the blessings and promises meant for Israel in the Bible.

After a while, the Lord led me to lay down my career in politics to serve Him on the mission field. For about two-and-a-half years, I had the privilege of spreading the gospel in Asia, Africa, and South America. Even as I thought my time in politics was a distant past life, I felt the Lord nudging me that I would one day return to the sphere of government as His servant.

I returned to the States for Bible school and joined a group called Youth with a Mission (YWAM). During my Bible program, I began studying the Bible in its historical and cultural contexts. I realized that much of the New Testament was written to Jewish believers. As I remembered my close Jewish friends from college and their disdain for Jesus, I wondered, *Where are the Jewish believers now?*

I still had three months left in Bible school, but I felt the Lord ask me to leave early, move to Dallas, and go on a trip with Him. I had no direction from the Lord other than to fly in and out of London between May 20 and June 10, 2019. I received a surprise $2,500 donation and waited on the Lord to show me the rest.

A TRIP THAT CHANGED MY LIFE

After I booked a flight, my friend Samuel asked if I would be interested in attending an event in Jerusalem called the Jerusalem Prayer Breakfast. This annual event gathers government, business, and ministry leaders from around the world to pray for peace in Jerusalem as Psalm 122:6 commands. It just so happened that it was taking place in the middle of the dates of my trip. So I went to Jerusalem.

I had two divine appointments during that first trip to Israel. The first led to a continuing role with Israel, and the second to a lifelong commitment. During the event, someone jokingly asked everyone under 40 years old to raise their hands. In a group of 700, there were about 25 of us. One of those under 40 was a man named Peter Griffin. A mutual friend insisted on introducing us at the conference and eventually set us up on a blind date. She described the man as someone who loved Jesus, loved missions, worked in finance, and lived in New York City. The minute I heard New York City, this Texas girl said, "No, thank you!"

She didn't take no for an answer and introduced us anyway. We had a wonderful first date, but I had no interest in starting a new relationship. The next day, however, Peter invited me to Yad Vashem. Unbeknownst to me, our second date would be at Israel's Holocaust Museum with his parents.

That same day I was praying while waiting at a bus stop, and I asked the Lord, "Why did you bring me to Israel?" At that very moment, I looked up and saw Allan Parker, who runs The Justice Foundation in San Antonio, Texas. Four months later, I started a new job at The Justice Foundation as their liaison to Israel. I also said yes to Peter's marriage proposal.

I traveled twice more to Jerusalem to work with pro-life Israelis on behalf of The Justice Foundation. I had studied biblical Israel in depth while at Youth with a Mission (YWAM), but my trips to Israel were a crash course on modern Israel and its many complexities. My project in Israel hit the ground running but then suddenly halted eight months later due to COVID. Peter and I exchanged our vows on Friday, March 13, 2020, while the pandemic was simultaneously shutting down the world.

LONGEST HONEYMOON EVER

We arrived at the airport to board our flight to Morocco for our honeymoon, only to learn the Moroccan border had closed. While trying to salvage our honeymoon, Peter prayed and felt we were to fly to Hawaii. We landed in Maui with our carry-ons, expecting to stay no longer than a week. Two days later, Hawaii shut down travel from the outside. We secured a $1.30-a-day rental car, and the owner of our condo insisted that we "stay as long as you can" and "pay whatever you can." Peter started working New York City hours from home, which meant waking up at 1:00 a.m. Initially, we enjoyed our extended honeymoon, but after about a month, we were desperate for friends.

In the second month, we met Robb and Nora Finberg, pastors on the island. Not only were they pastors, but they were of Jewish background. Rob, a Long Island Jew, and Nora, an Iranian Jew, had met on an elevator in Jerusalem when they were young. They became our closest friends during the first few months in Maui. Peter and I spent hours asking questions about the importance of Jewish feasts and traditions and Israel's role at the end of the age. We started a crash course on what Christianity looks like with its Jewish roots stripped away.

While COVID paused my work in Israel, I began researching church history to learn how and when the church left its Jewish roots. Someone recommended a book called *When a Jew Rules the World* by Joel Richardson. In it Richardson explained the different covenants (Abrahamic, Mosaic, Davidic, and New) in a way I had never heard before. However, the most impactful part of the book was his timeline, starting at AD 115. He showed the progression of how quickly small strains of supersessionism (Replacement Theology)[13] in the early church grew to become church-sanctioned antisemitism.

---

[13]"Replacement Theology [also called 'supersessionism'] rests chiefly on the idea that the whole or part of the Abrahamic covenant has been abolished, for it is this covenant that promises to Israel eternal ownership of the land of Canaan (Genesis 17:7–8). Once this 'promise' has been removed, the present-day restoration of Israel means nothing, and her only hope is in the church. ... only in Christ Jesus can there be salvation for Jews and gentiles alike (Romans 1:16–17). However, we do not believe that the promise of God in the Abrahamic covenant bequeathing the land of Canaan to Israel has been removed, and therefore, Israel's modern restoration to the land of Canaan is indeed fulfillment of that promise and constitutes a milestone on her 'way home' to her Messiah (Ezekiel 36:24–28)." Hedding, Malcolm, "Replacement Theology," www.icejusa.org/replacement-theology/

Antisemitism started small as certain early church leaders forbade Christians to eat with Jews and celebrate Passover. It quickly evolved to mandates of public identification, threats of expulsion or death for not converting, terminating property and civil rights, and church-sanctioned persecution of Jews. Richardson writes, "What began as a Jewish sect that welcomed in the gentiles soon became a gentile-dominated group that looked down with tremendous disdain upon any Jews who didn't convert to the Christian faith, fully leaving their Jewish identity behind." After learning about the Spanish Inquisition of Jews in 1492, I was not the least bit surprised when the timeline arrived at the Holocaust. It almost seemed inevitable, and I was grieved.

I spent months in shame, disappointed that my former church had led me astray with their belief in Replacement Theology. Paul's warning in Romans 11 struck my heart:

> But if some of the branches were broken off, and you, although a wild olive shoot, were grafted in among the others and now share in the nourishing root of the olive tree, *do not be arrogant toward the branches.* If you are, remember it is not you who support the root, but the root that supports you. (Romans 11:17–18 ESV, emphasis added)

LIVING DEUTERONOMY 24:5

Peter and I continued our extended honeymoon in Maui, and by month six, I started joking with him that we might live out Deuteronomy 24:5:

> When a man is newly married, he shall not go out with the army or be liable for any other public duty. He shall be *free at home one year* to be happy with his wife whom he has taken. (ESV, emphasis added)

Lo and behold, we did live out this verse. On precisely the one-year anniversary of our arrival to Maui, Peter received an unexpected job offer, and after 15 months on our honeymoon, we moved to Miami, Florida.

A NEW CHAPTER

When we arrived in South Florida, we realized our new state had the third highest population of Jews in America. Everywhere we went in South Florida, we saw expressions of Jewish culture. I had this unexplainable love and excitement when I saw *mezuzahs* on doorframes and Jewish families walking outside during Shabbat. Even my first friend in Miami was Jewish.

Because of my love and passion for Israel, I was eventually introduced to Susan Michael, the International Christian Embassy Jerusalem (ICEJ) USA Branch director. After meeting over dinner, we realized there was something more to our new friendship. Today I serve as the event coordinator for the ICEJ USA, as well as for the Jerusalem Prayer Breakfast Houston.

People will probably always ask me, "Why do you care so much about Jerusalem and Israel?" It gives me great joy to answer that question now. It's an open door for me to share about the first trip to Israel that forever changed my life, how I learned that Jesus was Jewish, how I met my husband in Jerusalem, and about my work for Israel. I welcome the question because answering it opens the door for me to speak about the Jewish roots of my faith—and why I will forever be a friend, defender, and lover of Israel.

Allison Ngo Griffin, a former Buddhist, worked for the Texas House of Representatives before a radical encounter with Jesus in 2015. Her first trip to Israel in 2019 to attend the Jerusalem Prayer Breakfast led to ongoing involvement with Israel. Allison now works for the Jerusalem Prayer Breakfast and the ICEJ USA Branch. She is married to Peter, who she met in Israel, and lives in Miami, Florida.

Generation Z

Born between 1997–2012

13

HOW ISRAEL SHAPED MY
WORLDVIEW AND ASPIRATIONS

Grace Keathly

Israel has been a constant in my life for as long as I can remember, although its meaning and relevance have developed quite a bit over the past 22 years. As a pastor's daughter, the significance of the people and Land of Israel was continuously highlighted but often felt distant and remained in my peripheral vision until my early teenage years. It wasn't until my family moved from the United States to Ra'anana, Israel, in October 2013 that the Holy Land moved to the forefront of my life. I was 13.

Upon arriving in Israel, all my preconceived notions about what the Land would be like were quickly overturned. I expected to see rolling sand dunes and barren land, but I was welcomed by a sea breeze from the Mediterranean, date palms, thriving cities, and the sound of parrots cawing. I was astounded as the past met the present in a kaleidoscope of religions, cultures, languages, and practices.

The sights and sounds soon became my family's norm while my parents worked and attended language classes, and my sisters and I went to school. I attended an American international school, and my sisters went to Israeli public schools. Here we were introduced to people from across the globe and learned about different cultural practices and worldviews. Over ten countries and eight religions were represented in my grade alone.

A SUMMER TO REMEMBER!

At first our lives were relatively peaceful as we lived our daily routines. But in the spring of 2014, the quaint existence I had known was disrupted by the kidnapping of three *yeshiva*[14] boys on their way home for Shabbat. We waited with bated breath over several weeks, praying and hoping with the rest of the nation that they would be returned to their families. Posters showing their names and faces were everywhere, and the hashtag "bring back our boys" was popularized. The day their bodies were found was a day of mourning throughout Israel. Broadcasts showed the mothers crying for their sons, and entire communities grieved alongside the families.

After the boys' funerals, tensions with the Palestinians escalated, leading to skirmishes and sporadic violence. Nervous energy percolated just below the surface for the next several weeks. Amid this new reality, I attempted to return to everyday life and finish my final semester of middle school.

That summer, I attended a *kenes noar* (Christian youth conference), which is a summer camp for young adults across the country. This was where I experienced a second major disruption in my otherwise peaceful pursuit of life in Israel.

One night at camp, several friends and I were walking around the perimeter of a baseball field after dinner. As we strolled along, my friend,

---

[14]A school for Talmudic study; an Orthodox Jewish rabbinical seminary; a Jewish day school providing secular and religious instruction. "Yeshiva." *Merriam-Webster.com Dictionary*, www.merriam-webster.com/dictionary/yeshiva. Accessed 10 Jan. 2023.

Bria, pointed to the sky and exclaimed, "I think I see a flare." We all looked up to see a red dot streak above the city in the distance. We were curious but not concerned, so we continued on our way. Everyone around us remained calm, so we didn't give it a second thought as we carried on with the night, celebrating Germany's victory over Brazil in the World Cup. Little did we know that flare was a rocket fired from Gaza.

As I was waking up the following day, however, a counselor abruptly burst through the door, yelling in rapid Hebrew. Everyone in the room leaped from their beds and sprinted toward the dining hall, bleary-eyed in their pajamas. I followed the group, a bit dumbfounded as to what was happening due to my limited understanding of Hebrew.

Upon exiting the room where we slept, I heard the piercing sound of a siren reminiscent of those I had heard for tornadoes during my childhood in Texas. A sense of dread filled me as I sat down in a cafeteria chair in a stupor. An English-speaking counselor explained that the sirens were in response to a rocket attack and that we were gathered in the dining hall because the bomb shelter was not large enough to hold everyone in the camp. I sat there in shock and confusion because this unknown threat felt all-encompassing.

Gradually, campers and counselors started playing music and singing, even as the sirens wailed. Though I couldn't understand all that was being said, and it seemed like the sirens would never cease, I felt supernatural peace wash over me. For the duration of that summer, the droning siren became all too familiar as it sounded in the middle of the night, early hours of the morning, and even as my family drove on the highway.

RELATIONSHIPS MADE ALL THE DIFFERENCE

Amid this unsettling season, my family experienced a unique sense of community. Local restaurants and vendors posted signs outside their shops, signaling that their shelters were open to the public in case of a siren. We formed new relationships with neighbors while sitting next to them in the stairwell of our apartment building, seeking shelter. We came together at all times of the day—sometimes in pajamas and sometimes with our hair dripping wet after having jumped frantically out of the shower. During those moments, my mind swirled with questions about why this was happening. But one thing I knew: the conflict I had heard of for so long had fully intersected with my own life.

During this time, my parents connected with a modern Orthodox couple from New York who were our neighbors. This couple became our cultural lifeline during our time in Israel, and through this friendship, my parents modeled for me what Jewish-Christian relations should look like. As they developed their relationship with our neighbors, my parents proceeded humbly and asked questions about cultural and religious practices that enabled us to be culturally aware and sensitive.

This experience opened a new world for my family, in which we were invited to Sukkot celebrations where we ate with several families in a *sukkah*,[15] attended a Yom Kippur[16] service at the local synagogue, and shared Shabbat dinners. In these moments, the Bible came to life. The feasts of the Lord were no longer just an ancient festivity, but they became for me a vibrant celebration and commemoration of the Lord's faithfulness and providence.

In these times of chaos and conflict, my family was welcomed into a beautiful community that taught me so much about my current reality and allowed me to engage with my faith in a new way. When we first arrived in Israel, we were students of the culture around us. But we soon found ourselves engaged in cultural exchanges through these meaningful friendships.

Interactions with our Israeli neighbors often involved holidays and food, and the American holiday of Thanksgiving was no exception. Every year for Thanksgiving, my family deep-fries a turkey. When we

---

[15] A *sukkah* is a temporary tent-like dwelling where Jews are supposed to dwell during the week-long celebration of *Sukkot*. These "tents" represent the huts the Israelites lived in while wandering in the desert after escaping Egyptian slavery. Sukkot, or the "Feast of Tabernacles," is one of the three pilgrimage feasts outlined in Leviticus 23 and is celebrated each year in the fall.

[16] *Yom Kippur*, or "Day of Atonement," is one of the three pilgrimage feasts outlined in Leviticus 23 and is celebrated just before Sukkot (Feast of Tabernacles) in the fall. It is considered the holiest day of the year on the Jewish calendar.

shared this tradition with our friends, they thought it would be wonderful to cook this dish for Hanukkah, when it is traditional to eat fried foods. So our neighbors taught my father how to *kasher*[17] a pot in which to cook the turkey, and he, in turn, taught them how to deep-fry the turkey. That Thanksgiving was a hilarious yet sweet blend of cultures. All these experiences caused me to fall in love with the people of Israel, and they have left a deep impression on my heart that continues to shape my worldview and aspirations.

ENCOUNTERING HATE

After leaving Israel, my family relocated to London, England, where I attended a secular international school within a synagogue. During my studies there, I applied a great deal of the knowledge I had gained during my time in Israel because several of my best friends were Jewish. We dialogued about our faiths and asked each other candid questions. I was honored to attend their Torah reading during our senior year.

In striking contrast to this amicable dialogue, I witnessed the defacing of the synagogue where I went to school and the resulting armed guards needed to provide security against antisemitic attacks. My heart broke as I saw such hatred firsthand. Unfortunately, my exposure to antisemitism did not stop there. I have seen it surge on my college campus and through online forums, sometimes quite blatantly. Other times it is thinly disguised in the form of anti-Zionism.[18]

PREPARING TO CONFRONT MISINFORMATION

My family returned to the United States in time for me to begin university. I chose to major in cultural anthropology due to my love for cultures, which developed through my experiences in Israel. This major, combined with my minor in global justice, kept me constantly engaged with the Jewish State.

---

[17]To make an item like a pot, oven, or pan *kosher* ("fit" to be used, according to Jewish law) by using heat to remove *unkosher* substances from the item.

[18]Opposition to the establishment or support of the State of Israel. "Anti-Zionism." *Merriam-Webster.com Dictionary*, www.merriam-webster.com/dictionary/anti-Zionism. Accessed 10 Jan. 2023.

As I considered how I would use my degree, I realized it boiled down to one thing: I want people—particularly younger generations—to truly learn who Israel is and be engaged in countering misinformation and antisemitism. One way I have done this is through my role as the social media intern with the US Branch of the International Christian Embassy Jerusalem (ICEJ). In this position, I have been part of young adult seminars, prayer calls, and promoting the work of the Embassy in Israel and abroad.

Working with the ICEJ has encouraged me immensely. I have seen this ministry build bridges with and serve local Israeli and Jewish communities, provide care for Holocaust Survivors, support education for minorities, donate bomb shelters for high-risk communities, and educate Americans about the importance of Israel today. This has fueled my passion for educating this upcoming generation about the reality of Israel and how to combat rising antisemitism.

My love for Israel and the desire to inform future generations has led me back to Israel, this time as a young adult. I am currently studying at Hebrew University in Jerusalem to earn a master's degree in human rights and transnational justice. I hope to combine my passion for social justice with a deeper understanding of Israel and the international legal system. I intend to advocate on behalf of Israel and work to strengthen Jewish-Christian relations at home and abroad for many years to come.

Grace Keathly is a graduate student at Hebrew University in Jerusalem and social media intern for the US Branch of the International Christian Embassy Jerusalem. Her awareness of Israel shifted to a lifelong commitment at age 13, when her family moved to Israel. Their firsthand experience of the national trauma following the kidnapping and murder of three yeshiva students in 2014 and the ensuing rocket attacks on Israel from Gaza led to the development of life-changing relationships with their Jewish neighbors.

14

NOT YOUR TYPICAL NINE-YEAR-OLD

Josiah Neumann

The whirling mind of an average nine-year-old often thinks irrationally and lacks maturity. It focuses on things like when they'll get their next snack or be able to swing on the monkey bars or play another round of video games. The average nine-year-old does not necessarily yearn for knowledge from his elders on a day-to-day basis or desire to read nonfiction material to understand historical events.

But I was not a typical nine-year-old.

I was raised in a Christian home where we read God's Word daily. My parents nicknamed me the "Old Testament Soul" because I was always drawn to Old Testament texts. The books of Kings, Esther, and Exodus are some of my favorites. I have always been in awe of the passion, level of faith, courage, and strength of the Jewish people whose stories are recorded in the Bible. As a child, I knew them all. I knew their names, their children's names, their wives' names—they were *my* ancestors! While most young children were watching television sitcoms, Marvel movies, and cartoon characters, I was obsessed with movies about King Solomon, Queen Esther, Jacob, and Joseph. These were my true heroes to emulate!

The average nine-year-old also does not have the opportunity to travel across the globe to the war-torn Middle Eastern country of Israel. But here again, my experience was not average. In 2014 when the Gaza War started, one of the deadliest outbreaks of conflict between Israel and the Palestinians, my parents still accepted an opportunity to travel to Israel with Bishop Robert Stearns and Eagles' Wings Ministries.

My father and Bishop Stearns were youth group friends and continue to share a deep connection to this day. Because of their close friendship, my parents were comfortable trusting Bishop Stearns and Eagles' Wings with their safety during this trip. And they knew it was not an option to leave me at home!

At nine years old, I was fully aware of the ongoing conflict between the Palestinians and Israelis. I found myself constantly watching the news on TV and social media. I understood the threat posed by ISIS and other terrorist groups in the area when we would be traveling. Even after returning from the trip, I continued to stay informed with updates from Israel regarding attacks by terrorist groups in the area and other relevant news.

Josiah on his first trip to Israel at nine years old, 2014

Unfortunately, the Gaza War of 2014 and ongoing terrorist attacks are not recent or new phenomena. The Jewish people have been persecuted and scattered among the nations of the world throughout history, and modern Israel's very existence is continuously threatened. However, for the first time in 2,000 years, the Jewish people have been reunited as a nation due to the creation of the State of Israel in 1948. Even though there has always been a Jewish presence in the Land, the founding of modern Israel marked the reestablishment of Jewish sovereignty in their ancient homeland.

Despite everything that has happened to the Jewish people throughout history, they still stand to this day. As a people, they have not wavered in times of trouble and turmoil but have maintained their faith and connection to God. Even amid the Holocaust, as they were on the verge of being wiped out by the evil Nazi agenda, many did not turn from their faith in God and trusted Him that better days were to come.

TWO PROFOUND IMPRESSIONS

That trip to Israel in 2014 left two indelible impressions on my life. The first has to do with my reflections on the Holocaust. As I stood in the Land, I wondered, *What was the rest of the world doing while this [the Holocaust] was happening to these people?* My next question was, *What needs to be done so this history will not be repeated?*

But my experience in Israel also caused me to realize how important it is for the United States to support Israel and protect the freedom she now holds. Before I experienced the Land of Israel for myself, I never truly understood the need to support the Jewish State. Even though my family had participated in events led by Bishop Stearns and Eagles' Wings Ministries, such as the Day of Prayer for the Peace of Jerusalem and Buffalo Celebrates Israel, my connection with God's chosen people did not truly begin until I stepped foot in the Land.

THE FAITH OF ISRAEL

While in Israel, I saw the Jewish people's dedication and passion for God—but God allowed me to preview this before I even arrived in Israel. While on the plane, I experienced something profound that demonstrated the commitment and longing to speak with God that the Jewish people live for. I was awakened early that morning by the sound of praying and crying out to God. I turned in my seat to see the entire back of the plane filled with young men praying and seeking God out loud. I was shocked—I had never seen anything like this! But as I began to understand why they were doing what they were doing, I connected with them on a spiritual level because I felt their desire to connect with God. For them, nothing else mattered except their relationship with God, and the deep hunger I witnessed was something I wanted too.

We were in the Land during the holiest time of the year on the Jewish calendar: Rosh Hashanah[19] and Yom Kippur. Watching the Jewish people celebrate those events provided a profoundly spiritual experience that would forever change me. I was in awe as I walked the desolate streets on Yom Kippur, streets that were empty as an entire nation observed the most holy day of the year. I was also incredibly moved from praying at the Western Wall with my father, Bishop Robert Stearns, and other men in our group. To stand in a place with such a rich history where so many generations had stood before us was humbling, to say the least. I carry these precious memories of Israel in my heart.

I am finishing my senior year of high school and will soon head to college to pursue a career in law, but my experience in Israel as a young boy will inspire me forever in my support of Israel. God willing, I hope to one day be a part of global meetings in which I can stand for Israel with my voice and pen. In the meantime, I stand with Bishop Robert Stearns and Eagles' Wings Ministries as a watchman on the wall in the calling to protect Israel (Isaiah 62:6).

Josiah Neumann is a senior at Grand Island High School in Grand Island, NY, and plans to pursue a career in law and political science. Josiah has a passion for history that began as a young boy while learning the biblical history of Israel. When he was nine, he went to Israel with his parents amid the 2014 conflict with Gaza, in which terrorist rockets were fired at Jewish civilians. As a result of this experience, Josiah ponders what the world was doing during the Holocaust and what must be done to prevent history from being repeated.

---

[19]The Jewish New Year. Jews observe this holiday on the first day (Orthodox and Conservative Jews also on the second day) of *Tishri* on the Jewish calendar.

15

A GENUINE FRIEND

Alyssa Ruddell

"Sounds like you had a lovely time and got to see some neat things," remarked a friend from back home as I excitedly relayed my recent experiences in Israel. I tried to share how incredible the trip had been and how it shaped my life, but she could not grasp the depth of its impact on my heart. How could she? She had never explored Israel's prophetic history, seen the Land, or met the wonderful people who call Israel their home. Yet I had—and it forever changed my life.

My journey to Israel began several years ago when my dad was privileged to visit the Land on a two-week assignment with the US Air Force and had an excellent experience meeting Israeli people. After that trip, as I was nearing the end of high school, he began studying prophecy concerning Israel in the Tanakh. (Tanakh is the acronym in Hebrew for the Pentateuch, the Prophets, and the Writings of the Hebrew Bible.) With excitement, he began sharing with me about Israel's significance in the past, present, and future—and his enthusiasm was contagious.

FANNING A SPARK INTO A FLAME

From that point on, I knew I wanted to visit the Land of Israel. An opportunity came the summer after my freshman year of college through an annual trip sponsored by my university. I was elated as I boarded my first flight to Israel in 2019. I soaked up everything like a sponge and was constantly in awe of everything I saw. I was especially keen on exploring sites from the Tanakh like Tel Dan, Ein Gedi, Hezekiah's tunnel, and Jerusalem because they carry such historical significance.

By the time I reluctantly returned home, the spark of interest I had in Israel was growing into a flame. I incorporated this experience into my academics as opportunities presented themselves. I was even asked to speak about the trip to encourage other students to visit Israel with the university at the next opportunity.

I also selected the topic of antisemitism and its unfortunate prevalence in society as one of my research presentations at my university. And in my final semester, I incorporated the importance of the Jewish people into my papers whenever I could. As a Christian, I know God's love and plan for Israel remains steadfast to this day—and I want other people to understand what that means.

ONE CLOSED DOOR OPENED ANOTHER TO ISRAEL

As I continued pursuing my nursing degree, my love for Israel's land and people grew in my heart. Then, an unexpected turn of events brought about an incredible opportunity to act on that love.

I had been accepted into several nursing programs but decided to apply to one more and was waiting for the acceptance letter. However, instead of a letter of acceptance, I received one of rejection. This development brought with it a season filled with confusion and much prayer.

During that same time, as I was finishing an online degree in health sciences, I heard about a free online class about Jewish customs and culture offered by the Friends of Israel. It was designed to enhance one's understanding of and love for the Jewish people. Since I already knew about this organization through their magazine *Israel My Glory*, I readily signed up for the BRIDGES program in the spring of 2022. I learned a lot about Jewish culture, festivals, history, and different denominations within Judaism.

After a few weeks, the course leader asked if I wanted to join their annual ORIGINS trip to Israel that summer. ORIGINS is an acronym for **O**ur **R**esolve **I**s **G**iving **I**srael **N**ever-Ending **S**upport. The trip is designed to provide young adults the opportunity to see the Land of Israel, and, more importantly, to volunteer and support the Jewish people. The trip—designed to blend touring with volunteer work— offered the perfect opportunity to return and give back to the Land of Israel. I could not have been more excited!

Because I was not in nursing school, I was not constrained by clinicals or other commitments. The bottom line was I could go on a trip I had always wanted to go on because I had been rejected from that nursing program. The timing for this amazing opportunity was impeccable!

Alyssa viewing the Sea of Galilee during the Friends of Israel's ORIGINS trip, 2022

Over the course of our 18-day trip we visited places like Jerusalem, Tel Aviv, the Sea of Galilea, Masada, the Dead Sea, and Caesarea Maritima. We volunteered with the national food bank, Leket Israel, where our team saw firsthand the ingenuity of the Israeli people—and we did our best to assist them in their work. We spent three days working at the logistics center sorting through fruits and vegetables, followed by five days picking *kohlrabi*[20] in fields near Rehovot.

Volunteering while interacting and building relationships with Israelis was such an enjoyable experience. And because of technology, several members of the ORIGINS team and I have remained in contact with our Israeli friends. Impactful in every way, ORIGINS strengthened and expanded my desire to support and love the Jewish people.

WHAT NEXT?

After returning to America, I knew God was leading me to do something with my heart for Israel. He had not given me these experiences, sparked these desires, or rearranged my plans without reason. Now I needed to pray about what to do next. I started learning Hebrew through texting with Israeli friends and other available resources. I longed to know more about the Jewish people and their stories, so I read biographies by Jewish authors, such as *Night* by Elie Wiesel and *The Search* by Lorna Simcox, which gave me important insight.

When I discussed my interest in supporting Israel with the staff of Friends of Israel, they were thrilled to discover someone who shared their passion. So my next step was to join their ENCOUNTER trip to observe the Jewish community in Crown Heights, Brooklyn, New York.

This trip provided incredible learning opportunities through events like walking through museums detailing Jewish history, visiting synagogues, and meeting wonderful people. When we toured historical

---

[20] German turnips; a biennial vegetable in the cabbage family.

synagogues, we were privileged to hear from rabbis and learn about their beliefs. I am so thankful God let me have all these educational experiences!

MY CALLING CONFIRMED

During the ENCOUNTER experience, God decidedly confirmed that my calling in life was to support and bless the Jewish people in some capacity. But how? Where should I start?

My next step was to apply for a three-month internship with the Friends of Israel, during which I began volunteering with various Jewish organizations in my hometown. At the same time, I connected with other college-aged students on campuses around the state to share with them the importance of supporting the Jewish people.

Since the fall of 2022, I have been exploring how I can serve, support, and love the Jewish community around me. So far, I have visited a Shoah Museum, made Shabbat boxes for hospital patients, and delivered meals to Jewish people in my hometown.

I also long to share my love for Israel and the Jewish people with churches and other Christians. Sadly, many do not properly understand how important Israel is or that the Bible teaches us to love and support the Jewish people. Unending in His love, God has never forsaken His covenant with Israel. The Torah makes that clear in Genesis 12 and 15, Leviticus 26:42, and Deuteronomy 4:31. It is undeniable: God will forever be in covenant with His people, and His heart's desire is to be in close relationship with them.

One thing my experiences have taught me is how much God can be trusted and how much He loves the Jewish people. I desire peace for the Jewish people and the Land of Israel and want to be of any help. Over the centuries, Israel and her people have undergone many difficulties and trials. Should a time come when I am called upon to protect, support, or stand up for Israel and her people, I pray I will do so without hesitation and with proficiency.

My earnest hope is that God would use my life as a testimony of His love for His precious possession (Deuteronomy 7:6)—and, as a result, the Jewish people will know that this Christian friend is a genuine friend.

Alyssa Ruddell recently earned her bachelor's degree and works as an intern with the Friends of Israel and as a volunteer with the Jewish population in Houston, Texas. Her life was changed forever during a 2019 trip to Israel, when she saw the Land, met the people, and explored Israel's prophetic history. A subsequent trip in 2022 with Friends of Israel solidified Alyssa's call to stand with the Jewish people, and she looks forward to continuing to serve, support, and love them through her work.

16

PROUD TO SUPPORT A COUNTRY THAT CHANGES LIVES

Hannah Delamarter

I was seven months old when America was attacked on September 11, 2001. Obviously, I do not remember that catastrophic event. But because of how the world changed after that day, I also do not remember a time of actual peace. I have particularly been aware of ongoing conflicts in the Middle East my entire life.

I grew up in a Christian family, and my Christian faith defines who I am. Growing up, I knew we supported the Jewish State, but I did not understand why. For me, Israel was a historical place because it was the land of the Bible, but I didn't put much thought into the significance of the existence of the modern State. That all changed when I went to college!

In my freshman year, a group of students from Christians United for Israel (CUFI) was fundraising for Save a Child's Heart (SACH).[21] I had not heard of either of these organizations, but my involvement

---

[21]Save a Child's Heart (SACH) is an Israeli humanitarian organization working internationally to save the lives of children from countries where access to pediatric cardiac care is limited or nonexistent.

with both changed the course of my life. Their work opened my eyes to the call God has upon my heart.

In 2021, when I was 20 years old, I stepped foot on the Land of Israel for the first time with a group of strangers who had signed up to go on a tour sponsored by CUFI. This is when the *why* behind my support of Israel became so clear.

MEETING MODERN ISRAEL

I had always dreamed of walking where Jesus walked when He was on this earth. And there I was, in the most war-torn region on the planet, perfectly safe and free to walk where He walked. Where else in the Middle East— including other countries with biblical sites —would I be safe as a Christian? Where else but Israel could I gather with Jews and Christians at such significant sites as the Western Wall? Where else in the

Hannah on the Sea of Galilee, 2021

Middle East would I be able to witness Muslims going to prayer without experiencing pressure to join them? I quickly realized that Israel was the only country in the Middle East where I was free to be a Christian.

In addition to the religious freedom in Israel, there is equality for women. There I was, a White, 20-year-old female in the Middle East, walking around in a t-shirt and shorts, and I was safe and welcome. I covered my knees and shoulders at holy sites out of respect for the sites, but everywhere else in Israel, I was free to dress as I chose with no fear of judgment or ridicule. I was welcome at all religious sites. I could talk to men without fear. My education and aspirations were encouraged and appreciated. In short, nobody treated me as "less than" because I am a woman.

I also had the opportunity to see the good Israel does for the world. I learned about the Good Neighbor Project, which gives aid to victims from war-torn Syria. I witnessed the work of SACH, which provides life-saving heart care and surgeries for children across the Middle East and Africa. I realized that Israel is a country that offers freedom and safety for all religions—and for women—and even extends help to those who wish it harm.

Israel is unique in how it welcomes and provides medical care for children from other countries—sometimes enemy nations—at no cost to them. Being surrounded by Israelis who long for peace, are not violent or hateful, and want to be safe in the Land promised to them— the Land where their forefathers lived—was a life-changing experience for me.

I left Israel a different person than when I arrived; I met a people determined to have peace who honor the promises of God. I walked where Jesus walked. I could not visit a place like that and not want to help it, preserve it, and do everything I can to support it. No one can extinguish the spark lit inside me from my experience in Israel!

Since I returned from the Land, I have been the president of my school's chapter of CUFI. My school's CUFI club is not large, but it effectively educates and advocates in support of Israel. We educate young Christians as to why we should pray for Israel and how important it is to ensure the people of Israel know they will never be alone. The education we provide is essential for counteracting the dehumanizing propaganda against Israel promoted on social media and informing and educating this newest generation of American voters.

In addition to my work with CUFI, I have led fundraisers for SACH—the other organization that introduced me to the wonders of

Israel. SACH is one of the noblest organizations I know of because it was founded on sacrifice and care for children from multiple countries. Learning about the work of this organization changed my heart and inspired me to live a life that values and protects others, even if it is of no benefit to me.

My experience in Israel did not produce a temporary love—I will always support and invest in Israel. I am pursuing a degree in nursing and hope to work at SACH upon graduating. No matter what, I will always share why I love Israel. I wholeheartedly support Israel because Israel provides me and the world with the promise of peace. It is a nation I am proud to support as an American. It is a nation I am proud to support as a Christian. It is a nation that has changed me and continues to change the world.

Hannah Delamarter is a nursing student at Northwest Nazarene University. When she was 20, Hannah went to Israel on a tour sponsored by Christians United for Israel (CUFI). The why of her support for Israel became clear as she realized that Israel was the only country in the Middle East where she was free to be a Christian—and safe and welcome as a woman. Since returning from Israel, Hannah has been the president of her school's CUFI chapter, which educates and advocates on behalf of Israel.

17

THE LAND THAT CHANGED MY LIFE

Nicholas Zanzot

As I gazed across the water with the wind rushing around me, I sensed God's presence more than I had at any other time in my life. In that moment, it was as though the wind was God's arms embracing me as I was welcomed into a holy relationship with Him. I had heard of spiritual moments like these from others who have traveled to Israel, but to experience something like this myself was surreal. For me, this happened while on a boat in the middle of the Sea of Galilee.

Reflecting on that day and remembering other occurrences that transpired while I was in Israel still makes me smile. My heart grows fonder of the Jewish State as each day passes, and because of the life-altering moments during my journey there, the calling from God that took me to the Holy Land has morphed into a mission to support the State of Israel forever.

A member of Generation Z, my connection with the Jewish State does not span decades or include numerous trips to Israel. In fact, it has only been six years since a calling from God right after my eighteenth birthday led me to this land.

Before starting at North Carolina (NC) State University in 2016, I lacked any genuine connection to religion and did not understand the significance of the State of Israel. Even though I was baptized as a child into the Christian faith, my upbringing included only occasional interactions with the church. While recognizing that religion may be important to others, mine was limited to attending church on Christmas, Easter, and other occasions (humorously classifying me as a "C.E.O."). My baptism as a baby gave me a foundation for faith, but it was not until I became a member of the "Wolfpack" at NC State that I truly accepted God into my life.

While attending university, many individuals and organizations—including the chief justice of North Carolina, Paul Newby, and volunteers within the Cru organization on campus (formerly "Campus Crusade for Christ")—helped "unlock" my door to Christ, who continually knocked from the other side, longing for a relationship with me.

As I reflect on this time, I cannot help but be in awe over God's magnificent plan. Like the creation of the Jewish State, where the miracles of God are present throughout its history, His hands are evident in my journey due to the people and situations I encountered along the way. As a result of the perseverance of God and the prayers of those in my life, I accepted Christ as my Lord and Savior during my freshman year of college.

MY NEXT STEP: ISRAEL

Because of how God began to speak to my heart about Israel, I knew my next step was to visit the promised land. My faith was strengthened by Proverbs 3:5–6, which instructed me to "Trust in the LORD with all your heart, and lean not on your own understanding; in all your ways acknowledge Him, and He shall direct your paths." With the goal of going to the Holy Land in mind, I started looking for a way to fulfill God's calling for me.

Soon after I started my research, I found the trip that would get me to Israel: the 2019 Arise tour with the International Christian Embassy

Jerusalem (ICEJ). The ICEJ is an organization that represents Christians around the globe to the Jewish State, and I could not have imagined a better group to guide me on this journey.

Nicholas atop Masada at sunrise during the ICEJ Arise 2019 tour to Israel

By God's grace—and with the support of family and friends—I embarked on the trip. While in Israel, I went from Eilat, the southernmost part of the State, to the peak of Mount Bental in the north, stopping at numerous places along the way.

Notably, my trip included visits to Timna Park, the Dead Sea, Masada, the Sea of Galilee, the Mount of Beatitudes, and sites throughout the holy city of Jerusalem. And on one of the most memorable days of my life, I was baptized in the waters of the Jordan River, just as Jesus Christ was two millennia ago.

Little did I know how providential the timing was for that 2019 trip to Israel. I had initially planned to visit Israel the summer after I graduated from undergrad, the summer of 2020. If I had waited until then, I never would have made it. As the world shut down due to the global pandemic, I was filled with gratitude toward God for having pushed me to travel to the Holy Land the year before.

Amid the sadness and horror of COVID, the magnificent strength of the Israeli citizenry was revealed to me. For the first time in most people's lives, those of us in the Western world were living in fear of something just outside our door. However, the people of Israel deal with this every day from the ongoing presence of terrorism. They are resilient, and I pray that I can exemplify at least a glimmer of this courage and faith after witnessing it firsthand.

A CALL TO SUPPORT ISRAEL

Since my trip, the calling to visit Israel has evolved into one of support. Support, to me, does not conclude with the mere utterance of a phrase or an occasional public display of affection. Both are important, but my vision for support goes further.

While in the desert one night before heading to Masada to watch the sunrise, a pastor who had joined the trip stopped me after our nightly service. Up to that point we had barely spoken, but he said he felt in his heart that in the future, I might help others begin a relationship with God. He asked me if I had considered religious service. While I did not feel this was in God's plan for me, I knew then that a new purpose in my life would be to help bring others to the Holy Land to further their relationships with the Lord.

Visiting the Jewish State and speaking with Jewish people who worked for years to return to Israel showed me just how impactful seeing the Land firsthand can be. The miracles God has bestowed upon Israel and its people are evident but can be seen more clearly by traveling there. That night, as I gazed upon the stars above the Holy Land, I promised God I would endeavor to bring people to this magnificent place for the rest of my life.

Because of my journey, I am also motivated to use my future career in ways that can meaningfully assist and support the Jewish State here at home. As an aspiring attorney, I intend to use my skills and abilities to help organizations that support the State here in America and around the world. With all my strength, I will continue to advocate for assistance and support for Israel, the Land that has changed my life.

I also plan to continue to be involved with the ICEJ as they represent Christians worldwide in our shared appreciation and love for Israel.

I am forever grateful for my experiences in Israel and the changes that occurred in me along the way. One day, I hope to lead others to the Holy Land so they can experience the same hope and grace I saw every day while I was there. With faith and continued reliance on God, I pray that millions more will travel there so they, too, can see for themselves the importance of supporting the Jewish State of Israel.

Nicholas Zanzot is an aspiring North Carolina attorney who will graduate from the University of North Carolina School of Law in 2023. In 2019, while pursuing his bachelor's degree at North Carolina State University, Nicholas traveled to Israel with the International Christian Embassy Jerusalem (ICEJ) on one of their tours for young adults. He has stayed involved with the ICEJ USA and plans to continue his support of the Jewish State in the years ahead.

18

ISRAEL CAPTURED MY HEART

Sarah Weiskopf

The Land of Israel has captivated my heart in a way that words cannot express.

The Jewish nation warmly welcomed this curious college student when I arrived with a mind eager to learn more and a heart ready to be filled with more compassion and love for others. I set foot in Israel without a clue as to what the scenery would look like or how different Middle Eastern culture would be from my own. I did not even know what Israeli food would taste like. As I walked through the entire experience, Israel transformed me from the inside out. There was never a moment that did not constantly amaze me and leave me in awe of my Creator.

I left my hometown in Colorado to fly across the world to go to Israel because of an invitation I received from a girl who was part of a discipleship group I led on our college campus. She told me about Passages, a nonprofit organization that takes college students to Israel to learn more about the Hebraic roots of their faith. That same day, without hesitation, I filled out the application to go to Israel. Little did I know how much that relatively simple act would change my life forever.

GOD'S PLAN WAS SO MUCH BIGGER

It seemed like a spontaneous decision in the moment, but God had a plan that was so much bigger than what I could see. I knew that Israel is mentioned throughout all of Scripture, but I didn't know the hope I would encounter in the Holy Land. I knew Israel's existence is rooted in historical and biblical artifacts, but I never expected the genuine love of the Jewish people that I would soon experience. In May 2022 I boarded a flight with my friend from the discipleship group, along with several other college students from across the nation. I had no idea what was ahead, but God surpassed my expectations. As I stepped off our bus for the first time, I immediately noticed Israel's stunning scenery. The waves of the Mediterranean Sea and the aroma of the salt air made me feel at home within the first seconds of being in the Land; the water is a beautiful aquamarine color. Everywhere I went, I was surrounded by an assortment of vibrant, blossoming flowers. The architecture throughout every city in Israel is unique and carries the stories of centuries. Every word inscribed upon city walls in Hebrew carries a significant meaning and purpose.

As we entered the Old City of Jerusalem, we witnessed an incredible bond that unites the Jewish people. We saw Israeli flags strung across the streets and the coming together of people of all nations and religions in this holy city. The golden Dome of the Rock shines brightly amid the neutral-colored buildings. Crowds of people walk from place to place while numerous cars travel to their next destination.

Sarah at the Sea of Galilee, 2022

There is such joy within the walls of the Old City—people singing, dancing, and laughing together, others praying. Music rings loud in the air, and people celebrate one another.

EXPERIENCING GOD IN THE LAND

In the middle of this busy city, I felt a holiness like no other. Even amid the chaos of tourists and merchants, a supernatural peace encompasses Jerusalem. The hills and valleys of this nation truly proclaim the greatness of our God. In every rolling hill, vast mountain, and deep valley, it is evident that the Lord is over all of it.

I witnessed rushing waterfalls in the middle of the desert. I tasted the "milk and honey" of the Land as I ate dates from the flourishing palm trees. I felt the smoothness of my skin after rubbing mud from the Dead Sea all over me. Israel is a small country, but there is such beauty in every part of its diverse geography. From the desert to the sea, from the mountains to the valleys, Israel is captivating to the eye— but more importantly, to the heart.

Traveling to the Holy Land radically changed my faith. I will never read Scripture the same again. I will never pray the same again. The way I worship our Lord and Savior was forever changed by those 10 days in Israel.

Being able to walk where Jesus walked on the way to the cross transformed me from the inside out. I experienced the same heat Jesus would have felt on His skin and the same breeze that would have swept His hair across His face. I sat silently in the garden of Gethsemane, tears welling up in my eyes, thinking about how my Savior sat in this same garden just hours before His crucifixion. I went on a boat cruise on the Sea of Galilee and was overwhelmed with the peace the Lord so graciously gave through His Son. I witnessed the rich history of Masada as I toured the ancient ruins of King Herod's palace. I stood in the Garden Tomb next to an empty grave, knowing that the Savior I worship conquered death once and for all. I read the Sermon on the Mount at the Mount of Beatitudes, picturing Jesus' disciples eagerly learning from their rabbi.

My time in the Land allowed me to tangibly "taste and see" the Lord's goodness (Psalm 34:8) everywhere we walked. Jesus was always on His way to those who were sick, broken, hurting, lost, lonely, and held captive by their sin. Imagining Him standing next to me as I walked the streets of Israel was surreal. Being in the Holy Land gave me a fresh perspective concerning Jesus' resurrection and the reality that I can live in relationship with Him on Earth and for all eternity in heaven.

MEETING THE PEOPLE OF ISRAEL

Not only have the geography, history, and biblical roots of Israel impacted me, but the people of Israel have too—they are such a blessing. Every person I encountered was full of boldness, passion, abundant care, love, and hospitality to the people around them.

One dear Jewish family welcomed us into their home to enjoy Shabbat dinner with them—a beautiful and unforgettable experience watching them celebrate the Lord's design for rest together in community. The streets are empty, people leave cars at home, and no phones are in sight. On Shabbat, markets are abandoned as people enjoy the simplicity of life alongside one another.

Israel truly understands what it means to stop, be still, and know that the Lord is God (Psalm 46:10). In America, we tend to pride ourselves on our busyness, but Israel takes the commandment of the Sabbath seriously and leans into the gift of rest. If Creator God, who made the heavens and the earth, took a day to rest and reflect on the goodness of creation, how much more do we need to do so as fragile humans? God does not require sleep or rest, and yet He rested. How much more important is it for humanity to rest so that we can function as God intended?

My heart continues to grow in love for the Jewish community every waking day. The Lord has revealed Himself to me through the Jewish way of life and through Judaism itself. Without an understanding of the Jewish roots of Christianity, my faith in Jesus would not be what it is today. Jesus was Jewish; understanding the Hebraic culture in which He spent His life doing ministry has opened my eyes to a much deeper understanding of my Christian faith.

A GROWING PASSION

I never knew I could become so passionate about a nation other than my own. I never realized how much my heart would grow to love and cherish people from another country. Since my return to the States, I have been listening to Israeli music, studying Hebrew, cooking Mediterranean food (even though it's not the same as eating *shawarma* on the Mediterranean Sea!), learning more about the faiths represented in Israel, and growing in my affection for the people of Israel.

I am on my way back to Jerusalem to study there for five or six months and dive deeper into Jewish studies, the Hebrew language, and Middle Eastern culture. I have a heart for caring for others and specifically for working in the nonprofit sector. Being able to witness the innovation and creativity that fills Israel is inspiring. Watching people's creative ideas come together to make Israel the "start-up nation" is a unique experience I will never forget.

Israel has my heart. No other nation is so theologically rich, rooted in thousands of years of history, and made up of people who genuinely care for their culture and customs in such a unique way. I am blessed to have set foot in the Holy Land and hope to be there again and again.

Sarah Weiskopf is a senior at Grand Canyon University in Phoenix, Arizona, studying business entrepreneurship. She has a deep love for Jesus and encouraging others. Sarah is the founder and president of Anchor of Love, a nonprofit for individuals with cancer. In May 2022 she went to Israel for the first time with Passages, and her faith and life were transformed by walking where Jesus walked.

— EPILOGUE —

You are invited to write a new chapter in your own life story by visiting Israel! These 18 examples of lives changed and passions ignited represent millions of Christians who have done so. You, too, can step into the story by contacting one of the organizations mentioned in this book and signing up for your trip-of-a-lifetime. Perhaps you are moved to help these organizations grow their programs that take young adults to Israel. It is the most effective way for tomorrow's Christian leaders to experience their Bibles coming to life and their faith ignited as they also come to appreciate the Jewish roots of their faith and the significance of Israel. Your donations to enable more young adults to go to Israel are encouraged. Below is a list of the nonprofit organizations in the United States that take Christian young adults to Israel as mentioned in these testimonies.

Bridges for Peace • www.bridgesforpeace.com

Christians United for Israel • www.cufi.org

Eagles' Wings • www.eagleswings.org

The Friends of Israel Gospel Ministry • www.foi.org

International Christian Embassy Jerusalem • www.icejusa.org

Institute for Black Solidarity with Israel • www.ibsi.org

Passages • www.passagesisrael.org

Philos Project • www.philosproject.org

—GET YOUR FREE RESOURCE TODAY—

Request your FREE downloadable resource *Top 10 Finds in Israel That Support the Bible*—and share it with family and friends. This full-color resource includes vibrant pictures and maps of some of the top archaeological finds in Israel that support the biblical account. You'll also be alerted when we release a new book, online course, or other educational tools.

—FREE DOWNLOADABLE RESOURCE—
www.icejusa.org/top10

—LEARN MORE ABOUT OTHER RESOURCES—
by Dr. Susan Michael at: www.susanmichael.com

—LEARN MORE ABOUT THE MINISTRY—
of the International Christian Embassy Jerusalem at: www.icejusa.org

—FOLLOW US ON—
www.facebook.com/icejusa
www.instagram.com/icejusa_1980

—LEARN MORE ABOUT—
ICEJ U online courses, books, and podcasts at: www.iceju.org

—CONTACT US AT—
embassy.publishers@icejusa.org

— ABOUT SUSAN MICHAEL —

 For more than 35 years, Susan has pioneered the development of the International Christian Embassy Jerusalem in the United States and around the world. She currently serves as the ministry's USA director and is a member of the ICEJ's international board of directors. In addition to a master's degree in Judeo-Christian Studies from the Jerusalem University College, she holds a bachelor's degree in theology from Oral Roberts University and was awarded an Honorary Doctorate of Laws by Piedmont International University in 2018. Susan is an author, gifted teacher, and international speaker.

She is often called upon to address complex and sensitive issues such as antisemitism, Jewish-Christian relations, Christian Zionism, and current events in the Middle East to a diverse range of audiences. Her experience working with Jews, Christians, and Arabs from many national and denominational backgrounds has equipped her to handle delicate topics central to an understanding of Israel with extraordinary clarity and grace.

In recent years she has produced several educational tools to enable other Christians to do the same, including the ICEJ U online school, the IsraelAnswers.com website, biblical study tours to Israel through ICEJ USA Tours, and Susan's Blog of over 200 articles and podcasts. Susan has built the US Branch of the ICEJ into a scripturally sound, balanced, and reputable ministry, evidenced in its leadership of one of the strongest networks of Evangelical leaders in America—the American Christian Leaders for Israel (ACLI).

— ABOUT EMBASSY PUBLISHERS —

Embassy Publishers is the publishing arm of the International Christian Embassy Jerusalem designed to introduce the Christian reader to the biblical significance of Israel and the Jewish people, the history of antisemitism, Jewish-Christian relations, the modern State of Israel, and Christian engagement with Israel.

— ABOUT THE ICEJ —

The International Christian Embassy Jerusalem was established in 1980 in recognition of the biblical significance of all of Jerusalem and its unique connection with the Jewish people. Today, it represents millions of Christians, churches, and denominations to the nation and people of Israel. We recognize in the restoration of the State of Israel God's faithfulness to keep His ancient covenant with the Jewish people.

Our goal is to stand with Israel in support and friendship, equip and teach the worldwide church regarding God's purposes with Israel and the nations of the Middle East, be an active voice of reconciliation between Jews, Christians, and Arabs, and support the churches and congregations in the Holy Land. From its head offices in Jerusalem, the ICEJ reaches out to more than 170 countries worldwide, with branch offices and representation in over 90 nations.